WRITING:
"IT'S IN THE BAG"

WAYS TO INSPIRE YOUR STUDENTS TO WRITE

BY

MARGARET TAYLOR STEWART

Crystal Springs
BOOKS

A division of Staff Development for Educators (SDE)

Peterborough, New Hampshire

Published by Crystal Springs Books

75 Jaffrey Road

P.O. Box 500

Peterborough, NH 03458

1-800-321-0401

www.sde.com; www.crystalsprings.com

Library of Congress Cataloging-in-Publication Data

Stewart, Margaret Taylor.
  Writing : "it's in the bag" : ways to inspire your students to write /
by Margaret Taylor Stewart.
     p. cm.
Includes bibliographical references (p.   ) and index.
  ISBN 1-884548-41-5
  1. English language—Composition and exercises—Study and teaching
(Primary) I. Title.
  LB1528 .S76 2002
  372.62'3—dc21

                                         2002003864

Editor: Sandra Taylor

Design and production: Soosen Dunholter

Photography: Margaret Stewart

Author photo and student artwork: Courtesy of Margaret Stewart

ACKNOWLEDGMENTS

I am indebted to the many people who have contributed to this book in various ways. I have learned from every child who has been in my classes over the years; from fellow teachers who have shared their ideas and suggestions with me, who have allowed me to observe their instruction, and who have pondered with me about the best ways of working through problems; and from administrators who allowed me to create classrooms built on my beliefs and ideas. I have learned from professors who have challenged my thinking about language, literacy, and ways we come to know about our world and from the words of writers and thinkers they have had me read. I thank Maryann Manning for supporting and challenging my learning throughout my graduate years, particularly in the realm of constructivism, reading, writing, spelling, and integrated aspects of literacy. I thank Jerry Aldridge for all he taught me about theory, thinking, and writing, and for encouraging me to transform this manuscript from its beginnings as a workshop presentation into its present book form. I thank Gary Manning for all he taught me about writing—both children's writing and my own—and for encouraging me to read Ralph Peterson and to investigate classroom community in my own classrooms. I thank Meredith O'Donnell for reading and making suggestions for this manuscript during the beginning stages of editing. I especially thank Sandy Taylor for her long hours, insightful comments, and suggestions as we finalized the text.

To my wonderful mother, Virginia Campbell: I appreciate your time, unceasing proofreading, and positive feedback at all stages in the process of creating this book. To my husband, George, and my daughters, Ginna and Amy: I appreciate your encouragement in seeing this book through to the end.

DEDICATION

This book is dedicated to the many children with whom I've enjoyed learning . . .

especially Ginna and Amy.

M. T. S.

TABLE OF CONTENTS

 INTRODUCTION

This book is written as a personal account in which I offer ideas that I've compiled over the years about writing with young children. These are not presented as *the* way to write but as *a* way to write with them. Drawing from my own experiences as well as those of other teachers, I have included here the most useful and practical "teacher-tested" strategies that have helped many young learners experience success in writing.

As a teacher—both in my own first-, second-, and third-grade classrooms over the 26 years I spent in those grades and now, in other teachers' K–3 classrooms, in which I work with *their* young students—I have been entrusted with the often daunting task of instructing young writers. At times I have felt inadequate about tackling such an overwhelming responsibility, and I have had concerns about the best ways to teach children to write. But I know that, for me, the very best way is to do exactly that—to have them *write!*

Because there *is* no one best way to teach children how to write, I feel strongly that each of us must discover what works best in our *own* classrooms, year-by-year and student-by-student. And I am confident that by doing so, our approach to writing will not be static but will vary each year as our students change and grow.

This book is designed to offer suggestions, to share types of writing that have worked well in my classrooms, and to encourage you to pursue your own ideas. Chapter 1 addresses concerns that teachers have about writing with their young students. Chapter 2 deals with strategies for writing with young children. Chapter 3 shares different formats for writing with young children. Chapter 4 explores writing from literature. Chapter 5 discusses writing from experience. And Chapter 6, the concluding chapter, focuses on literacy across the curriculum, described as a "balancing act." It includes a discussion of the need to balance philosophical considerations and administrative edicts within a practical format. Attention is also given to balancing curriculum considerations and time constraints. There are suggestions for making writing conferences manageable in classrooms of very young children and for making ongoing assessment an integral part of the teaching process. The appendixes provide selected children's literature listings, suggested readings for teachers interested in learning more about writing in their classrooms, purchasing and construction information for materials mentioned in the text, and forms that assist in managing the literacy practices described here.

Writing with young children is challenging but also rewarding and exciting! Don't wait until you're an "expert" to begin. Start today!

CHAPTER 1

ADDRESSING TEACHER CONCERNS

Writing can be approached with dread or with enthusiasm. As a teacher, it has been my experience that whichever of these attitudes I have held, my students have held also. Consequently, the way I feel about writing is very important and *does* directly affect my students. I am committed to incorporating writing in my classroom in as many ways and for as many purposes as possible. I also strive to make the writing experience a positive one for students as we work together to connect all aspects of language in meaningful ways. The purpose of this book is to share these ways with you, but before exploring them, I'd like to address some of the concerns teachers often have about the process of writing with young children.

Over the years I have heard about—as well as experienced—many of the roadblocks that prevent teachers from including writing in classrooms of very young children. Following are some of these concerns along with my suggestions for overcoming them.

CONCERN SUGGESTION

I am not a good writer myself, so how can I teach my students to be good writers?

I just "jump in" and learn along with the children. Thinking about what helps me as a writer, I know that the initial step for me is finding a *topic* about which I want to write and really have something to say. I try to help students find an area for themselves in which they have sufficient interest—as well as ample confidence in their expertise—to discuss on paper.

I try to capitalize on the students' enthusiasm for what they know a lot about or have experienced. I try to find interesting places to take them so they will have much to tell. When this is not possible, I share a book that I really like with the children and let my enthusiasm for the book spill over into helping them write their own versions of the story. I find that my own attitude—whatever that happens to be at the time—is reflected in almost every student's writing efforts.

CONCERN   SUGGESTION

My students do not know how to begin writing.

To combat this way of thinking I try to scaffold, or support in many ways, the children with whom I write. I do this by letting those who need extra support tell their stories on tape for me to type later. I let them work with partners who are stronger in writing. I do shared writing with them; that is, they write as much as they can, then I write a bit for them, letting them share the pencil as often as they will. This seems to give them added confidence. Many times I have struggling writers come to me as soon as they write a sentence so that I can write a "translation" in conventional English while they can still remember what they have "written."

I also find that complimenting children on their illustrations strengthens their texts. Many children write best when they first "draw" their story. Once they have the picture(s) done, they have something "concrete" to write about—something that they can study to find details that they might otherwise neglect to tell.

Many times I act as a scribe for students who need that extra support. Sometimes I draft volunteers—grandparents, parents, friends from civic groups, students from other grades, stronger writers from my own classes—to act as scribes as well.

In addition to having children journal and write stories individually (from the first day), I usually begin the year by writing with them in many settings and for many purposes as a whole class and in groups of four or five until they understand how to go about writing a story. I try to model good writing. I also try to think aloud so they can follow my reasoning. I talk about several ideas, making choices among them and discussing *why* I keep some ideas and dismiss others.

CONCERN   SUGGESTION

My students say they don't have anything to write about.

My answer to this is to give students some experiences. I read predictable books to them for sharing and rewriting. I take them on field trips or on "expeditions" around the school (to the playground, lunchroom, office, etc.), and together we write about what we saw. At first we write as a large group, then in small groups, and throughout the process as individuals. I ask them to tell me about their personal interests. I also try to get them to pick a topic for a picture book or journal entry that they know something about, such as their cat, their dog, a trip, their brother, their mom, their favorite food, etc. I do this to help them realize that they have stories of their own to tell. We consistently share our stories with each other.

CONCERN   SUGGESTION

My students are too young to "really" write. I worry about their spelling.

I find that when I don't expect perfection, I am much more easily able to see the gems embedded within children's work. By accepting approximations toward conventional spelling, I encourage students to value what they know about the way language works and to take ownership of as much of the system of spelling as they can, as quickly as they can. In other words, I accept the "temporary" (or "invented" or "phonetic") spellings that children use in first-draft writing, discussing with them what they have *right* in that word. I have students work first on conveying meaning to their audience—then I work with them to help them acquire conventions of writing. We move toward using sources of spelling, such as word walls, familiar books, dictionaries, and the help of peers to make our later drafts conventionally spelled. (Read more about spelling in Chapter 2.)

CONCERN   SUGGESTION

My students make too many mistakes.

I tell the children that it's OK for their first draft to be messy—that, in fact, I *prefer* to see words inserted, lined out, circled, etc., so that I can see their thinking, their choices, and their revisions. I have found their work becoming dynamic and stronger. Whenever I see children making mistakes and growing from them, I think of Ferreiro and Teberosky's (1979) discussion of the power of constructive errors in the processes of learning. These researchers investigated ways very young children come to know written language. They learned that children use problem-solving strategies as they grow in literacy. The children go through levels of progression in which they learn from their errors as they move closer to adult conventions about written language. "These are *systematic* errors, not errors due to lack of attention or memory" (page 17; emphasis added).

I no longer agonize over children's mistakes or consider them poor reflections upon my teaching. Instead, I am excited by them and use them as my "window" into the mind of each child as he or she learns and grows. I talk with children about ways in which all of us learn from our mistakes and about how we can use our mistakes as "steps" in the process of growing. When they become aware of an error in their writing (or reading or speaking) and attempt to correct it, I ask them, "What did you do that good writers [or readers or speakers] do?" Invariably their confident reply is, "I went back and put in a better word [or the word I left out, or a word that makes sense, etc.]." I always smile and give an enthusiastic, "Yes!" I view mistakes as opportunities for growth and I go to extreme lengths to teach students to see them as such.

CONCERN SUGGESTION

My students hate having to rewrite every story because of mistakes.

Personally, I don't think they *should* rewrite every story—for *any* reason! I do not see that it is important for every writing effort to be perfect. There is a place for first-draft writing in many school situations every day. I usually have children keep their stories in their writing folders. Later, they may decide to revise them, or they may just reread them to see how much better their writing is now than it was at an earlier time.

CONCERN SUGGESTION

When my students edit their stories, my room is in chaos.

I usually try to stagger the process so that not all students are at the same stage of the writing process at the same time. I have learned to schedule some children to begin new stories; some to reread all selections in their writing folder in order to select a piece to publish; some to work on illustrations; some to read for background information; some to proofread and edit independently; some to read their stories to peers; some to work with me on final editing; some to prepare their final, polished, completely correct draft; and some to share finished pieces with other classes. I schedule brief, individual conferences as needed at various stages of the process. I work with small groups of students when they have a common need, scheduling group conferences as necessary. I also make use of peer conferencing.

CONCERN  SUGGESTION

I really can't stand the mess my students make when they write.

I usually begin by trying to help students become more organized. I have each student bring one folder for works-in-progress and another for completed pieces. We keep these in two crates in specified areas of the classroom.

ORGANIZATIONAL HINT:

Writing folders are color-coded so that I can be sure I've read at least one-fourth of them after school each day (or—more likely—each night!). I read them to evaluate the children's writing progress, to determine who needs help, to look for common problems as topics of mini-lessons, to look for strong pieces to share, and so forth. The folders are arranged alphabetically by last name and then numbered so students can easily return them to the correct spot and a student "manager" can quickly check off the folders for me and remind classmates to file their writings.

Folders should be color coded: ¼ red, ¼ yellow, ¼ green, ¼ blue.

CONCERN SUGGESTION

I would like to use peer conferences, but my students are cruel to each other.

My answer to this problem is to work toward establishing a bonded classroom community in which students genuinely care about each other and look for the good in each other's work. This requires much attention and hard work and does not happen overnight. Before this comes about, I have students share stories with the whole group as I point out the *good* things about each piece of shared writing. I tolerate no "put-downs." I express personal enthusiasm for and enjoyment of the author and the writing. Once this "search for the positive" is in place for group sharing situations, I find that it carries over to peer conferences as well. Generally, the peer conferences quickly become patterned on the strategies I use in whole-group and individual conferencing.

CONCERN SUGGESTION

I would like to spend more time on writing, but I have to cover the skills curriculum.

I find that by introducing and integrating as many skills as possible through literature and/or writing, I usually am able to accomplish much more instruction than when I was so intent on "coverage" of the material. More important, I truly feel that the "learnings" the students carry with them from these integrated, authentic experiences with various applications of text are much more meaningful and long-lasting than much of what students from my earlier classrooms carried with them.

As I observe students, I find myself becoming aware of how much more thoroughly they grasp concepts presented in context. I like to use Dorothy Strickland's (1998) model of skills instruction ("whole-part-whole") to introduce skills as part of a meaningful whole, to focus in-depth instruction on that skill, and to re-situate the skill in the meaningful context of the whole. For example, I might create a story about a personal experience that happened outside of school, modeling for the children as I think aloud and write (creating a *whole* text). I would deliberately include a particular mandated skill topic, such as compound words. I would have the children go back and reread the story with me, looking for places where we find "two words that go together to make one word." When we found them, I would then do a direct instruction lesson on that topic—in this case, compound words (learning about a *part* of written language text). Then I would have the students reread the entire text with me, raising a finger each time we read a compound word so that they would notice the new skill (compound words) in the context of a *whole* text. If time allowed, I might then have them apply this new skill to their own writing by asking them to create their own *whole* text containing compound words. For me, this model makes wonderful sense as a basis for a balanced approach to literacy instruction and will, perhaps, allow the "pendulum swings" of theory (that so heavily impact practice) to still or, at least, slow down.

It is helpful to set aside time each day for writing. Because this seemed impossible when I first started teaching this way, I began by finding time at least every other day. As I became more comfortable with teaching through integrated instruction, I gradually increased the time, and I now teach through writing every day and in every subject area.

CONCERN SUGGESTION

My students complain about having to cover so much space on the page.

I find it helpful to use a variety of formats for writing. I use "flip books" and "step books" to get a quick overview of a child's grasp of a subject without requiring a lengthy written response. I also make half-page journals that seem to be much less intimidating to young writers, especially at the beginning of the year. These techniques are explained in more detail in Chapter 3.

CONCERN SUGGESTION

I like to have my students write in journals, but if I don't respond to them, they become discouraged about writing.

I usually begin the year by having students write in half-page personal journals every day on any self-selected topics in which they have a personal interest and want to share with me. I respond by writing a note back to each one every day. I can usually keep that up for about two weeks! After that I have them write during set intervals—for example, on Mondays, Wednesdays, and Fridays for one reporting period, or on a daily basis for a two- or three-week period. At that point I usually promise to answer them at least once a week. I let them write in subject-specific logs or in brief reflective journals in which they respond to specific questions from me on the other days. As the year progresses, this type of free-choice journaling on personal topics takes a less prominent role in the overall focus of writing in my classroom, but it is very productive at the beginning of the year. It works toward establishing a bond between the students and me. When these early personal journal entries are shared (as children often ask to do), with the "good things" pointed out, not only is writing strengthened, but also connections are forged between and among children as they experience snippets of each other's lives. (See Chapter 3 for more details about journal writing.)

CONCERN  SUGGESTION

My students work at such different speeds that it's hard for me to manage my classroom when they're writing.

I try to talk with my students about the importance of using time wisely. Those who finish are allowed to read their stories to another class, to make a duplicate book for the school or classroom library, or to begin a new writing effort.

Sometimes I suggest that they read a book, listen to a particular taped story to see how that author expressed ideas, or examine illustrations to gain ideas for their own illustrations of future books. Although some learning centers lend themselves to use during this writing workshop, I do not recommend having children do more lively activities during this time as it often causes others to rush through their writing efforts in an attempt to get on to the "fun stuff." For me, it has worked best to have all the children working on some quiet writing, reading, or other literacy activity at this time.

CONCERN SUGGESTION

My students hate to write.

When my students tell me that they hate to write (which is more frequent when they first come into the classroom), I try to find out what their interests are. I sit with them and ask questions to probe their thinking about a subject they know well. I try to support them in their writing as they are getting started, whether by acting as their scribe, by allowing them to dictate their words into the tape player for later transcription by me, or by allowing them to work with a friend. I look for the strengths of their work and give them opportunities to share what they have written or dictated. I try to be an enthusiastic listener and actively encourage them in their writing. I also encourage the other children to point out the "good things" about that person's writing (or drawing or attitude). The children and I can usually find at least one strong point in each student's work. From that good beginning we encourage the individual to build on the positive and stretch to take risks in writing.

CHAPTER 2

ENCOURAGING YOUNG WRITERS: PRACTICAL STRATEGIES

Although the physical plant of the school in which I teach is old—built in the 1940s—I work hard to make our classroom a warm and welcoming place, where children immediately know that reading and writing are important parts of our lives together. At the beginning of each year, I set up the classroom in a way that invites children to read and write. I arrange books on shelves, line them up on windowsills, place them in baskets on top of tables, fill discarded greeting card racks with them, and rest them on chalk trays. In fact, I have books on every available surface! Because it's very important that children see print wherever they look in a classroom, I have printed matter of many kinds, including charts, poems, and songs, displayed throughout the room.

As the year progresses, we fill our word walls with words we use and need. Our window shades proudly display the group stories we write together. Our writing overflows into the hallway outside our classroom door as we post daily notes and stories about our observations and experiences. Invariably, on the first day of school, when I ask my students what they can tell about me, they respond, "You really like books!" That is just the opening I need to start them on our year of shared literacy experiences.

In addition to pictures of storybook characters and a few puppets sitting around the room, I also have a collection of drawstring bags on top of my filing cabinet. If anyone asks me about the bags, I try to keep them a mystery, saying, "Oh, those are *special* bags. You'll find out about those today!" Then, sometime during that all-important first morning, I make a point to pick up each bag with care and take it to a low table in the middle of the room, bringing my collection to a central focal point. I make sure that this takes me many trips, so that by the time I have moved every bag, all the children are watching to find out what will happen next. I invite my students to come to the floor to sit by me, being sure that the bags are visible to everyone. The stage is set. I am ready to introduce my young students to writing. I begin by telling them something like this:

"Writing reminds me of a drawstring bag. When we open a bag, people just *automatically* want to see what's inside. A story beginning should be the same way—it should make people *want* to see what's inside. Some stories are soft, like this velvet bag; or comforting and special, like this bag made from my grandmother's quilt; or wild and exciting, like this glitter bag; or funny, like this clown bag; or filled with imagination, like this rainbow bag; or mysterious, like this question mark bag. But they are *all alike* in that someone put his or her *thoughts* inside. That person gathered many ideas together and wrote them down to share with others. That's exactly what *we* are going to do this year!"

At that point, I usually pass around the various drawstring bags my mother made for us so that the children can open and close them, peek inside, feel the various textures, and closely examine the patterns and sizes of the bags. I purposely asked my mother to make the bags as different as possible in order to quickly make my point with the children that although they are all drawstring bags, they are all very different—each one unique in its own way. With this example, the children can easily visualize a story as being different from many others but still a story, nonetheless. This simple activity also allows me to talk about "opening" a story and "drawing a story to a close" in later conversations about writing. Since I have been introducing writing this way, my students have seemed to more easily grasp the concept of situating their readers in their stories before just "jumping into" their tales. It has allowed me to talk about various ways of ending stories—as different ways of "closing our bags." This technique has been easy, fun, and particularly effective with very young writers. (A pattern for one of my mother's bags appears in Appendix A. It may be enlarged, widened, or used as is to create bags for use in your own classroom.)

Use Strategies for Teaching Writing

The following ideas are intended to nudge your *own* creativity and are not meant as a prescription for every classroom. I hope you will use what appeals to you and what you feel will work well with *your* students. It is important for children to associate reading with writing and to see the interconnectedness. Children who perceive themselves as authors are empowered in *every* area of the language arts.

Introduce Writing Workshops with Mini-lessons

I find it helpful to gather the children around me so that they anticipate the lesson. This prepares them to enter the world of writing as well as brings them physically close to me so that better rapport is established in the classroom. It also is easier to catch a student's eye if he or she begins to disturb other listeners. Sometimes a look or a pause when teaching can help the students remain focused. I try to keep lessons short (about 10 minutes) and to the point.

Writing workshops, as described by Graves (1983, 1994) and Calkins (1986), are extended blocks of time during which children are allowed to write (see Appendix B for a resource list to read more about this). One format for these workshops is to begin with a 5- to 10-minute teacher-led "mini-lesson," which briefly makes a point that is applicable to all—or most—of the students and is relevant to what they need in their writing at that time.

For example, I like to call the students together, read several picture books to them to point out a particular feature for them to emulate—such as including captions and labels in nonfiction texts—and then send them off to various places in the room to write, telling them to try to include captions and labels in their own nonfiction picture books. The mini-lesson is usually followed by an extended period of time—usually 30 to 40 minutes—during which the children are engaged in some phase of the writing process. Following that, I call the students back together to share several pieces of writing from that morning's workshop—usually for 10 to 20 minutes. (If for some reason we are unable to share then, we find time for it later in the day. The sharing seems to be a *key* element of this process.) Using this format helps children begin with a focus, remain actively engaged in their writing, and learn from each other's successes and mistakes. Mini-lessons are also effective in moving children forward in the processes, as well as conventions, of writing.

Although mini-lesson topics are best developed for particular groups for *their* specific needs, you may wish to incorporate some generic topics that most young children need, such as:

STAYING ON TOPIC

Explore picture books with the children to see how the author kept to the subject or to see ways the illustrator highlighted particular details of the story so that pictures and text match on every page (see Chapter 4).

"FRAMING" SENTENCES

Jan Norris, a professor at Louisiana State University, in a 1999 guest lecture to one of my literacy classes, discussed an easy but effective strategy. Early in her lessons for struggling readers/writers, she has the children "draw" their stories first as a series of pictures, "framing" each picture by drawing a separate box around it. She follows this by having children write a sentence to "draw" in words what is happening in each picture. Then she has them "frame" each sentence with a capital letter at the beginning and a punctuation mark at the end. I have used this procedure with young children since hearing about it and have shared it with my student teachers and interns, who have found it easy to teach and extremely helpful to their own students. It is the most effective way I have ever seen to have young children visualize beginning sentences with capital letters and ending them with punctuation marks.

USING "BETTER" WORDS—SYNONYM SEARCH

Show students how to search their drafts for "little" words or "weak" words that they can change to make their writing stronger (e.g., replace "big" with "huge" or "enormous" or "massive"; replace "cold" with "icy" or "frigid" or "frosty").

USING PROOFREADING MARKS

Show children several useful and common proofreading marks to help them make changes in their writing without erasing or copying over excessively. Here are some that are appropriate for this age group.

- caret for insertions: ^

- line through word for replacement: ~~big~~ huge

- three lines under letters needing to be capitalized: ann

- circled word for word spelled differently than it would be spelled in a book: (bote)

Although there are other proofreading marks they can learn, these four simple ones help students become familiar with editing their own work. I generally add others as needed, depending upon the age and experience of the students.

USING SCISSORS AND TAPE TO "CUT AND PASTE" A STORY INTO BETTER ORDER

After copying a teacher-written first draft, actually cut it apart and switch the sections to make better sense. Tape the story back together so the children can see that even teachers sometimes have to rearrange the order of their written pieces to make them better. It is often laborious for young children to rewrite their pieces, so cutting and pasting helps them have a good attitude about revising.

Note: Following the introduction of this editing strategy, place the original story and the "cut-and-pasted" version side by side on a "draft board" to remind students of this procedure. (A draft board is a bulletin board on which there are examples of various ways to edit stories, such as using proofreading marks, examples of cut-and-pasted stories, and so on.)

USING TAPE TO "ADD ON" TO A STORY

Tape a story elaboration (an addition to a story) to the side of a piece of writing, near where it belongs. Number the sections so that the original beginning is #1, the elaboration is #2, and the section of the original piece that now should follow the elaboration is #3. Add this draft procedure to the draft board also, and suggest that children who discover other good editing strategies put up examples so their classmates can use and refer to them. It is important for children to feel a responsibility for coming up with good ways to revise their writing, not just depend on the teacher to do so.

WRITING FROM LITERATURE AS A "SPRINGBOARD"

Refer to Chapter 4 for ways to use literature in a mini-lesson format to give children ideas for their own writing.

PLAN BEFORE WRITING

It is important that children think before they write, and there are many effective ways to encourage them to do this. Sometimes, as a lead-in to the writing, I gather students together to brainstorm about our experience or our idea for a story. We handle the brainstorming session in many different ways. Sometimes we simply make lists; other times I draw webs or Venn diagrams on the overhead or board and the students do the webbing or diagramming themselves. Sometimes we do KWL charts (Ogle 1986). One chart tells what we *know* about a subject, another tells what we *want to know,* and the third is reserved until the end of the study when we tell what we have *learned.*

Another simple yet effective strategy that has worked well for me is a "quick check." I find that the five minutes this takes gives my children time to think through what they want to write and to commit to that decision before they begin. I ask them simply to raise their hands when they know what direction their writing will take. They tell me the topic and the format of that writing, which I jot down beside their name on my clipboard list. (Or sometimes I choose either the format or the topic and let them choose the other.) The children have the freedom to come to me during their writing workshop, when I am between conferences, and revise what they have told me they would do. If they do not revise, then I expect their written effort to be on the topic and in the format they reported. A sample of the "quick check" form I use is given in Appendix C. (I ask the follow-up questions shown when children share their writing or at their conferences.)

STAY CURRENT ON STRATEGIES FOR TEACHING WRITING

As teachers, we must understand these strategies ourselves before we can teach them to our students. I do not believe that we have to know *everything* about the writing process, but we should be reading about it and exploring it with the children. The more we do so, the better we become at scaffolding those behaviors. It also is necessary to build a strong foundation for ourselves by turning to authorities in the field who have studied and written about this for years.

Teach Stages of the Writing Process

The stages of the writing process are based on the work of Graves (1983, 1994), Calkins (1986), and others who have written extensively in this area. I have included a brief, generalized description of each stage, followed by a list for quick reference. For a more thorough treatment of each part of the process, refer to sources cited in Appendix B.

In the *prewriting* stage of the writing process it is important that writers—whether students, teachers, or others—actively think and plan for writing. Even after leaving this stage, we come to it again and again as we expand our projects. This is what Graves (1994) currently refers to as a place of beginnings, of choosing a topic. This involves unconscious and conscious *rehearsal*, or preparation for writing. This is a very important phase of the writing process, especially for young writers as they are learning to compose. Brainstorming as a group is often a good way to help children become familiar with this process.

The next stage of the writing process is the *drafting* stage in which we begin to jot down our preliminary ideas. In many cases research is required before the drafting can be completed. If so, we do the research, then write; if not, we simply write our first drafts. This is the stage in which ideas are more important than conventions of writing. This is the time to get thoughts committed to paper, not the time to worry about spelling and handwriting. Graves says that the common composing pattern that all writers use is this simple one: "select, compose, read; select, compose, read" (1994, page 80). This makes sense. Writers decide what they will write, compose (in their minds and/or on paper) what they want to say, and then read what they have said, deciding to make changes or going on to select the next aspect of what they will say. For all writers, this process of selecting, composing, and reading is not the same. Different writers attend to those phases differently—but each writer uses those steps to get through the process of putting ideas on paper.

At some point writers move to the *revising* stage, in which we try to improve our drafts, working on the sense of the story, the flow of our ideas, the wording and order of our sentences. At this point writers are still selecting, composing, and reading. We select a portion of our working draft to read; we decide how we can make it better, composing ideas and words for doing that; and then we read again to see how effective our revisions have been. Revision can be read as "re-vision," which literally means to "re-see." As writers, we want to look again at our drafts—to reflect about a page or a text, to think about other options, and to decide if what we see on the page is what we intended to convey. If there is a discrepancy between what we have written and what we meant to say, this is the time to work further on getting our message across so that readers will understand what we mean.

The most important aspect in getting children to revise what they have written is that they thoroughly *know the topic* about which they are writing. Also important for revision is having a sense of the *audience.* Very early on we should be helping children become aware of who will listen to or read what they have to tell. Sharing is crucial for helping children revise. It not only allows children to get feedback from the group, but also gives them a chance to hear their ideas as they read aloud. This is immensely helpful, especially to young children, for recognizing things that do not make sense, words that are left out, or times that they put in the same word too many times.

Graves (1994) encourages teachers to set up conditions that invite writers to revise. He specifically mentions giving *time* to write—at least four out of five days—so that writers stay connected to their work. When they break their involvement with writing for a day or two, they have to reorient themselves to their thinking, to what they were trying to say. Graves speaks of *interviewing students* about their writing in chunks— having them choose four pieces of their writing to discuss with you. His questions and comments to guide children in their thinking about their own writing are found on pages 227–228 of *A Fresh Look at Writing.* Basically, he suggests asking children which of the four pieces they feel best about, confirming what you've noticed that delights or interests you, having them point out specific parts of that piece that they like, telling you which pieces did not turn out as well as they wished, and saying whom they were thinking of as they wrote the preferred piece.

There are other direct elements that encourage revision, according to Graves, one of which is helping students gain a sense of their options not only when writing, but also at other times of the day, in other subjects, and in the ways they generally function in the classroom. He suggests reinforcing this sense of having options by interviewing students. For example, at the beginning of a piece, ask students what will happen next; in the middle of the process, again ask them what will happen next. If they face a problem, ask them what they can do if they're stuck; at the end, ask them what they plan to do with their piece now that they are finished (page 231). Encourage students to decide if they will share that piece with the group or with a friend or family member, publish it in some form, or keep it in their writing folder for future consideration. By interviewing children individually and often regarding their options, we are teaching them to know that they have them. I encourage teachers to read *A Fresh Look at Writing*.

We teach our students as writers that when they are satisfied that they have the content right, they move to the *proofreading/editing* stage, in which they look for errors in grammar and other mechanics and make needed changes. When they are sure that their drafts are as good as they can make them, they have peer conferences and/or teacher conferences for final proofing. Children who are writing every day for many purposes can not be expected to revise, proofread, or edit everything they write. If they are writing at a desired volume—that is, writing consistently and producing a quantity of pieces for various purposes—it is impossible for you to respond to everything they write. They are writing first drafts constantly, then *selecting* some pieces that are important enough to them to take to publication. In those pieces, the revision of ideas is of higher priority than the revision of the mechanics. However, it is important that students learn the conventions of standard English and that they progress toward including those conventions in their writing.

For very young children (kindergartners and first graders) I suggest working on ideas first, then attending to one skill at a time for corrections. It makes sense for them to learn to add on (or elaborate), to stay on the topic, and to improve in "framing" sentences with a capital letter and a punctuation mark. For older students (second and third graders and beyond) other conventions of writing, such as use of quotation marks for dialogue, paragraph indentions, and other grade-appropriate skills, should be introduced and expected.

It is very helpful to give children an editing checklist so that they are checking for specific types of corrections. The list they use should fit their needs and the time of year in which it is being used. Following are ex-amples of some skills that might be appropriate at various levels, realiz-ing that it is best to start with a few items for young children and gradu-ally add others as the children gain experience in writing.

Kindergarten example. Teachers should use district guidelines for expectations specific to their school setting and grade level. Good resources are the position statements of professional organizations, national standards, documents, etc.

- ☐ My ideas make sense.
- ☐ I framed my sentences with a capital letter and an ending mark.
- ☐ I listened to the sounds in the words I wrote.
- ☐ I looked at the word wall to help me think about spelling the words I know.
- ☐ I used the word wall to be a "Spelling Detective," using the words I know to help me figure out new words.

First-grade example. All of the kindergarten skills plus other grade-appropriate conventions of writing, such as:

- ☐ My ideas are in the right order.
- ☐ My telling sentences end with periods.
- ☐ My asking sentences end with question marks.
- ☐ My sentences with strong feelings end with exclamation marks.
- ☐ I started people's names with capitals.

Second-grade example. All of the K and 1 skills plus other grade-appropriate conventions of writing, such as:

- ☐ I looked for places where I could use stronger words.
- ☐ I indented at the beginning of each paragraph.
- ☐ I used quotation marks to show what someone said.
- ☐ I started names of streets, cities, and states with capitals.
- ☐ I used commas when I needed them.

Third-grade example. All of the K, 1, and 2 skills plus other grade-appropriate conventions of writing, such as:

- ☐ I was careful to give readers enough information so they can really understand.

☐ I looked for ways to add detail to my writing.

☐ I varied my sentences.

☐ I used dialogue in stories.

☐ I used commas in the right places.

☐ I used abbreviations correctly.

Attend to conventions of writing one at a time so that a child is not bombarded with everything at once. It is far better for a child to learn something well, put it into his or her own writing consistently, and then move on to another skill and fully understand it rather than to try to think about so many different skills that he or she becomes confused. It is also important for teachers to be good "kidwatchers," as Yetta Goodman (1985) puts it, so that we know which children can handle more skills and which need fewer at a time. This should be individualized for the child's needs and level of performance at the time.

The last phase is actually *publishing* writing or presenting the projects in some finished format. Again, this final phase is not required for every piece of writing that a child does. For pieces that are important to children and that they have selected to carry forward to a final form, several options are available. Teachers may decide to type stories for their students (or to have volunteers, parents, or older students do that for them). Children may be adept enough at using a computer to type stories for themselves. Children may write their stories neatly in a book format, as a poster, or as a story on chart paper or other special paper for display in the room or in the hall. Teachers may write the finished draft for children and let the children draw the illustrations or select the photographs to accompany the text.

In whatever format you and the child determine is most appropriate for that piece, make sure that the final draft is neat, conventionally correct, and appealing to readers. This should be a product of which the child can be justifiably proud. Whether this polished piece is bound or otherwise completed, sharing it in some public way is essential. This validates a student's hard work and enables him or her to experience the pleasure of authorship. Many times in my classes I have found that when one child creates an outstanding book or poster, it ignites other children's writing, often resulting in a "rebirth" of writing for that class.

It is important for children to view all of the phases in the writing process as interactive and recursive, rather than linear in sequence. Good writers move back and forth between phases as often as necessary to feel satisfaction with their finished piece.

QUICK LIST (based on the 1994 work of Donald Graves as a reminder of the *processes*—not the precise *order* or *timing*—of writing):

Voice—not one distinct phase of the process—totally permeates all phases of writing and gives uniqueness to what writers have to convey and how they say it

Prewriting—rehearsal—beginnings of composing: sometimes conscious; sometimes unconscious; may involve daydreaming, doodling, listing topics or words, sketching, webbing, outlining, reading, discussing ideas with others, "brainstorming," etc.

Drafting—selecting, composing, reading; selecting, composing, reading; . . .

Revision—literally "re-vision" or seeing again: involves reflection, paying attention to gaps between what we intend to say and the words as they appear on the page; is enhanced by sharing aloud with an audience (especially for very young children)

Proofreading/editing—finding errors and correcting the mechanics of writing

Publishing—producing error-free final copy of the work, ready for public sharing in some format

Even though there are various phases of deliberation and action in the writing process, Donald Graves (1994) cautions teachers against determinedly taking children through a set sequence of choosing, rehearsing, composing, and rewriting. He says that teachers must be cognizant of the writer's *voice* in the entire process, allowing that voice to convey to us a child's potential. Graves strongly cautions teachers against "legislating" the precise timing of the process of a child's writing. One of our biggest challenges as teachers of writing—or of any other subject, for that matter—is examining the potential of our students and setting appropriate expectations of them as learners. We challenge students best by setting high expectations that are based on real knowledge of them as learners and of the subject matter involved. The way we obtain that knowledge is by studying our classrooms, looking closely and carefully at our students and ourselves—all of us learners and teachers together.

Use Strategies to Keep Enthusiasm High for Writing

It is important that many of the children's writing efforts be finished, published pieces so they experience the entire process frequently throughout the year. However, because this process is so taxing for young writers, I do not think it should be required of every piece, as this could make children dislike writing. Instead, providing numerous opportunities in the classroom for first-draft writing is a very effective way to help children remain enthusiastic. For example, when the firemen bring a fire truck to our parking lot, I ask the children to write about what they learn, and I give them choices about how they will do that. Some may choose to make a poster. Some may write a bi-fold book, a step book, or a flip book (see Chapter 3). Others may choose to make a picture book.

When we study temperature, we keep notes of our findings so that we can create graphs, charts, and posters. When a performance is brought to our school, we write notes inviting family members. When we need science supplies, we write notes asking parents to donate leftover common household items. When someone has a birthday, we make impromptu cards for that person. I literally have my students write about *everything they do!* The following have worked well in my classrooms over the years.

- Act as a scribe for children.
- Model writing for children, talking through your thought processes.
- Teach children to value what is good about their writing.
- Teach children to strive to have their writing make sense.
- Look for approximations of conventional writing, not perfection.
- Show children where to look for spelling support.
- Create whole-group and small-group stories.
- Allow partner writing projects.

(continued)

- Give children choices in as many ways and for as many purposes as possible.

- Provide opportunities for children to write in every subject area.

- Have children write daily (in some type of journal or log at the beginning of the year; in other, more complex formats as the year progresses).

- Have children keep writing folders for storage of writings-in-progress.

EMPHASIZE THINKING—THEN SPELLING

While we almost always go through the first four stages of the writing process, we do not always publish. There are many instances in which great growth can occur for children without publishing every piece. There are times when we make lists, take notes, or write a first draft without ever having to come back to it again as a finished piece.

I ask my students to spell words the best way they can in rough-draft writing, encouraging them to circle words they are unsure of in the attempt to get them to express their thoughts without undue worry about spelling at first. Then I have them look over their drafts, checking to see if they have omitted words or need to add words or change them to have their story make sense. After that I ask them to check to be sure that they put periods and capitals where they are needed. Next, I have them try to find a source for correcting spelling.

Most of my second graders have become proficient users of dictionaries by January or before. They usually begin looking in the easiest dictionaries first but will doggedly continue through two or three other dictionaries on progressively higher levels of difficulty until they find the entry for which they are searching. When they come to me in frustration as they try to find a word, especially if they are having to use a harder dictionary, I try to help them find it for themselves. Other spelling options for them are searching for words around the classroom. We invariably have displays on tables and bulletin boards with labels to explain the content. Word walls are built on sections of the wall so that they are easily accessible. Books are displayed on card racks so that covers may be read and referred to for writing. Children have access to books that contain the words they need to use in their writing. They may retrieve their journals from the clear shoebox in which they are stored if they think of an entry that has a word they need to check. Posters on the backs of bookshelves, on walls, and in the hall have easily spotted words.

The children are also free to confer with peers about spelling, and I ask them to come to me as a last resort. If they *do* come to me, I ask them what other ways they have used to try to find out how to spell that word. I try to scaffold my students' spelling (Dorn, French, & Jones 1998) by asking them predictable questions so they can learn to ask themselves those same questions. For example, I might tell a child, "Say the word aloud and listen to the sounds." Then, "Tell me the sounds you hear." If they are saying the word "cat" and tell me they hear "t," I'll ask, "Where do you hear the 't'?" If they don't know it is at the end, I might say, "You're right. There is a 't' in the word 'cat,' but the 't' sound comes at the *end* of 'cat.' " Then I help them sound out the word, letting them write as they sound. When they have spelled the word by sounds, I usually write the word correctly on a card, place the card next to their written attempt, and let them compare how close they came with the sounds. I *always* compliment them on the parts of the word they are able to sound, even if it is only the beginning sound. This is a lengthy process, especially at the beginning of the year, but it is a rewarding one as the children quickly gain confidence and begin taking risks with their spelling.

Teaching children to pay attention to families of words *(-at, -et, -ip,* etc.), helps them become much more adept at spelling in their own writing. We constantly "collect" families of words in our room to make patterns of spelling that make sense in the contexts of our reading and writing, often incorporating those families into our various word walls. Wagstaff's (1999) *Teaching Reading and Writing with Word Walls* is an excellent, reader-friendly resource for teachers who would like to know more about ways to use word walls to build literacy skills.

The power of using *onsets* (letters before vowels in words and syllables) and *rimes* (letter "chunks" containing vowel and successive letters in words and syllables) for building vocabulary—both in reading and writing—is discussed by several well-respected authorities (e.g., Moustafa 1997, 1998; National Research Council 1999; Snow, Burns, and Griffin 1998, Strickland 1998). I like to have the children work from our word walls using onsets and rimes to generate lists of words that they can spell.

For example, if they can spell "ball," then they can also spell "hall," "fall," "call," "wall," "stall," etc. I put just *one* of those words to represent its "word family" on the Word Families Word Wall so that it doesn't become overly cluttered and difficult to use. I put whichever one of those words we have made a connection with through our work with poems, songs, stories, or other experiences with using words. From that word, the children are able to become "Word Detectives" or "Spelling Detectives" and build other words by changing the onsets.

I have students talk with me a great deal about sounds of letters and words as we work together to express our thoughts on paper. Many times particular spelling problems crop up in the writings of several children, acting as a springboard for more in-depth study of those spelling patterns by the class as a whole. Spelling is one area in which I constantly find uses for Strickland's "whole-part-whole" concept of balanced instruction, which was explained in Chapter 1. For a more detailed explanation, see Strickland's text *Teaching Phonics Today: A Primer for Educators* (1998). Another particularly helpful resource is the *Scholastic Guide to Balanced Reading K–2: Making It Work for You* (Baltas and Shafer 1996). This easy-to-read text provides a theoretical base and recommended instructional techniques in the area of literacy, as well as practical examples of ways to apply those ideas in the classroom. Although brief, the book is well worth reading, especially for those new to a balanced literacy program.

In spelling, as in other areas of writing and learning, I am much more concerned with what the children *can* do than what they *can not*. I want to study their first-draft writing to understand where they are in their processing of thought and language. I want my students to work to convey their complex thoughts. Writings of children who are willing to take *risks* in spelling are much stronger than those who are worried about having every letter correct at the first attempt. Children can learn to overcome spelling difficulties by constant effort and attention to good sources of spelling as they proofread and edit. If they attend to spelling *ahead* of content, often the piece is weaker, with less ownership and pride felt by the writer. Strong thoughts, logical order, and good word choices are our goals.

Teach Skills in Context

By teaching skills in an authentic context teachers allow their students to see the purpose for each skill and its relationship to the whole piece, thus increasing the likelihood of the student's using that skill in the correct context again at a later time. For example, teaching a mandated skill in an authentic context occurred when my students learned to write friendly letters to thank the lunchroom manager for our tour of the cafeteria. Simply copying a letter from a text would not have had the importance that their friendly letters had for the students. They *wanted* to write their letters in the correct format because they were sending them to a *real person* for a *real purpose*. Almost every student gave a close approximation to conventional letter form on the very first try. I attribute this to their *purposeful involvement* with the authentic context and their *ownership* of their letters (see Figure 1).

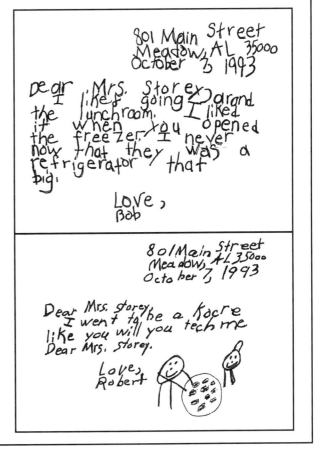

Translation:

Dear Mrs. Storey,
   I liked going around the lunchroom. I liked it when you opened the freezer. I never knew that the[re] was a refrigerator that big.

   Love,
   Bob

Translation:

Dear Mrs. Storey,
   I want to be a cook[er] like you. Will you teach me,
Dear Mrs. Storey?

   Love,
   Robert

(Picture is Mrs. Storey teaching Robert to cook pizza!)

Figure 1. Translations of first drafts of letters to lunchroom manager.

WRITING: It's in the Bag—

Other opportunities for authentic skills instruction often come as children read and share their written pieces with the class. I invariably point out the strengths of each piece, making sure I give verbal recognition at the end of the sharing for each correctly included skill, whether the skill is in the realm of comprehension, composition, mechanics, or grammar. Within a few weeks, many students are able to point out those same strengths in pieces written by their peers. After noting the correctly included skills, I always point out one (sometimes—though rarely—two) areas of needed improvement. I choose the most glaring error and give specific instruction for correcting it, and then ask the child to correct it at that moment. Taking advantage of such "teachable moments" in my classroom has had very positive results over the years.

ENJOY BENEFITS OF SHARING

A good way to strengthen both grammar and spelling, as well as other mechanical aspects of writing, is to have the students *share* their pieces. If the classroom is a safe place where a student feels free to share without fear of being ridiculed or teased when he or she makes miscues, students constantly grow in their manipulation of the processes of writing. This is not to say that typical writing by very young children is conventionally perfect or that the process is a quick one. Children need time, modeling, practice, and feedback in order to progress in their writing. Cambourne explains some "Conditions of Learning" that he sees as essential to classrooms in which teachers want students to flourish and grow in their literacy efforts—both in writing *and* in reading. He lists those conditions as ". . . immersion, demonstration, engagement, expectations, responsibility, use, approximations, and response" (Brown and Cambourne 1987, page 26). *Immersion* refers to having extensive print sources accessible to children. *Demonstration* means that teachers *model* reading and writing in front of children, thinking aloud as they go through those processes so that children see how a person problem solves in reading and in writing. *Engagement* refers to children's active involvement in the learning process in which they think of themselves as readers and writers, have real purposes for using reading and writing, and feel safe making attempts without fear of risk or embarrassment. *Expectations* of the teacher are important to children's learning and set the tone for what is accomplished in the classroom and beyond. It is important that the children are bonded with

40

the person who has set the expectations so that they will want to accomplish them. *Responsibility* refers to the teacher's expectations that the children are decision makers in their learning, make choices in their reading and writing, and are held accountable for engaging in the learning as they try to accomplish the learning task in a responsible manner. *Use* speaks of time and opportunity for children to use and gain control over the processes and skills that they are learning in real settings for real purposes. *Approximations* of children are important "windows" on children's processing that allow teachers to see how children problem solve about language and make progress toward adult conventions of language. In this area it is important that teachers look at the levels and types of errors a child is making and how the child is learning from his or her constructive errors. *Response* refers to the feedback that a child receives from a teacher or other person to whom he or she is bonded. The response affirms the value of the child's processes and products of language. Cambourne says, "Response must be relevant, appropriate, timely, readily available, non-threatening, with no strings attached" (page 26).

As often as possible I try to have children share their writings with the class. Sometimes time becomes a factor, and the children have to share with a peer or with me whenever they can snatch a minute during the day. I have found the sharing to be an essential component for optimum growth in students' writings. In my classroom, sharing is usually conducted on a volunteer basis, with almost every child clamoring to share every writing. If the sharing sessions become too unwieldy, I see that each child gets to share something at least every other day.

In Summary

By setting in place some predictable strategies, teachers can support young children as they learn to write. Children are successful when teachers use strategies such as the following as part of their regular classroom writing routine:

- Use drawstring bags to help children visualize the process of "opening" a story so that people want to see what's inside and "drawing a story to a close."

(continued)

- Introduce writing workshops with mini-lessons to make focused teaching points.
- Teach children to plan before writing.
- Understand the strategies for teaching writing using a process approach.
- Teach children the stages of the writing process and that they are recursive and interactive.
- Model writing and thinking about writing.
- Script for children when necessary.
- Emphasize thinking, and then spelling and other mechanics.
- Teach skills in context.
- Take time to share each other's stories.
- Look for and talk about the "good things" in each writer's work.
- Give each child one helpful suggestion to consider for the next written effort.
- Celebrate each child and his or her success.
- Allow the children to encounter—and share—writing as an enjoyable experience.

CHAPTER 3

SUPPORTING YOUNG WRITERS: A VARIETY OF FORMATS

WHOLE-GROUP AND SMALL-GROUP STORIES

I have found over the years that varying the formats for writing with young children increases their productivity. Two effective ways that I've used to model writing are to have them create whole-group and small-group stories based on their interests. These are wonderful formats to employ at the beginning of the year when the students are not sure what their new teacher expects of them.

First, I gather the materials. Chart paper measuring 24" x 32" is particularly good for this activity because it is long enough for a story to be developed to some degree, but short enough to be completed in a 10- to 20-minute block of time. I also keep on hand several dark, water-based markers that are full of ink to use as I script what the children dictate. (Water-based markers won't bleed through the paper.)

I provide illustration paper (8½" x 11" sheets of photocopier paper cut into halves or quarters) for every child who will be participating in the writing. When I am acting as a scribe for my students, it is very helpful to have each of them working on an individual illustration for the story. This gives each child something to be actively involved with while waiting for a turn to share an idea about the story. It also allows each student to feel that he or she is contributing even though he/she might not have the opportunity to actually add a sentence to this particular story. For the whole-group format, I hang the chart paper from the chalkboard; for the small-group format, I place it on a table where the students gather to write.

When I write with the whole class, I usually begin by asking, "What would you like to write about today?" Invariably, there are many responses to this question, which provides us with an ideal opportunity to begin learning how to make group choices. Normally, as the children make suggestions, I list each one on the board along with the name of the child (or children) who made it. When no more choices are offered, I ask the children to vote.

ORGANIZATIONAL HINT:

With young children, sometimes it is hard to get an accurate vote by a show of hands as they tend to raise their hands multiple times or change their minds. In order to take as little class time as possible for voting so we can get to the actual writing, I ask the children to move to a particular spot in the room to indicate their choice. For example, I might say, "If you want to write about our fall festival, go to the door." Then I wait a moment for the children to physically move to that spot. "If you want to write about football, go to the window." Again I wait for the children to move to that spot. This procedure works well for several reasons: First, the children are given purposeful movement immediately before a relatively lengthy immersion in a concentrated drafting session; second, it forces children to quickly take a stance on the issue—to make a choice and stand behind it; third, it allows them to visualize the voting process as an active choice between options; and last, it allows them to see that if their particular choice is not selected, it is not a personal rejection of them or their ideas, but rather the result of a group preference for another topic. I explicitly tell the children that if their idea is not picked this time, they might want to add that topic to their personal list in their writing folder or to consider getting some of their friends to join them later to write about their topic with me as a small group. I always make sure to follow through with this option at another time. (Although I realize that personality and peer pressure contribute to the whole-group topic selection process, I do not worry about it in this context. I feel that a quick selection is important, but I also make sure that other opportunities are given so that every child feels his or her ideas are valued in the scope of our group writing.)

By leaving the selection topics and names on the board and recording the number of votes cast beside each topic, I am able later to have the children create charts and graphs to illustrate our choices. For example, on one day, five people voted to write about football, four voted to write about cheerleading, six voted to write about Halloween, and seven voted to write about our fall festival. As the children moved to various places in the room to record their votes, I wrote the topics on the board with the names of the children who voted for each topic. We could easily see that the group wanting to write about the fall festival won the vote. Later in the day the children created a bar graph to show our voting. Each day that week we voted for large-group writing topics, recorded the information on the board, and created bar graphs to show our choices. At the end of the week we made a class book using some of the children's graphs as illustrations.

The process of recording votes and using them later to make graphs helps children have a purposeful use for making and reading charts and graphs, while at the same time underlining the process of making choices in a group situation. Once we have done this several times, I stop making the charts and graphs, but I always record the choices on the board as a reference during the selection process. It helps diminish arguments or hurt feelings. We do not *always* vote on a daily basis. Sometimes we write about our first choice one day, our second choice the next, our third choice the following day, etc. Occasionally we pick a writing topic and spend the week writing on different aspects of that same subject. However we choose our topic, I help the children find a fair, systematic way to go about it so that the students do not get the idea that their suggestions were "not good enough." I also frequently remind children that even though the group might not have selected their topic, they are certainly free to use it themselves. This has been helpful for some students who might be somewhat reluctant writers and who are looking for "something to write about."

Once we choose a topic, the children and I "brainstorm" about it before we actually begin writing. For example, on the day we voted to write about the fall festival, I asked the children to think of a good way to "open our bag." Several children had ideas that I jotted on the board in the form of a web because I wanted them to learn about making webs. In a central circle I put the words "Fall Festival." Lines connected that large circle to five smaller circles arranged around it. As students called out ideas, I wrote them in the smaller circles. When all five were filled, I told the children that we had enough ideas to write about on our short chart paper, so we stopped with that particular brainstorming session.

Once we have engaged in prewriting as a group, I ask the children to begin thinking about how their illustration will fit in with our story. Then, when we begin writing, I ask them to begin illustrating as well. I ask for someone to give us a sentence to "open our bag." Usually several hands go up for the opportunity to share an opening sentence. Because I feel that this is a particularly important part of our story, I call on someone who is a "good thinker" (not necessarily a "good student" in the traditional interpretation of the words). I make sure to vary the individuals I call upon so I do not always use the same student.

This process of writing with a group sometimes involves carefully helping children pick and choose among ideas by thinking aloud with them. I try to maintain a delicate balance between using their sentences exactly as they are dictated and helping them focus ideas so that the story will ultimately make sense. When the flow begins to wander, I start the next sentence with a word or two of my own to keep us on track, and I remind the students of the topic we have begun. I call on someone to reread what we have written so far, and I give the children options about the direction in which we can take our story. For example, I might say, "We've said that we saw some interesting things at the fair. What would make sense for us to say next?" After we get a new sentence, I'll say, "Now we need to go back and reread our story to be sure we know where we're going with it. Who can read it for us?" Occasionally I let several students reread if they are very focused on doing so.

Once in a while our stories begin in one direction and rapidly change course. This is generally accidental, but it gives me the opportunity to talk with them about deliberately changing the direction of the story so that it will hold a surprise for the reader. Some of our stories are factual and informative, others are ridiculous and funny. Whatever we actually create together, the overall outcome for our classroom is positive in several ways. The students have worked together (with each other and with me) to create a real story that all of us can "read" with some degree of expertise. This authentic document is displayed in a prominent place inside the classroom—such as clothespinned to the window shades—or in the hallway outside our door to remind us that we are real authors and illustrators . . . *and* real readers. We are developing a respect for thinking about writing and ways to express our ideas that will be meaningful to our readers. We constantly pay attention to our "audience," taking time to discuss how our readers are likely to interpret our story, thinking about points that need to be clarified for them, etc. We are actively immersed in the writing process together—at the same time and in the same piece. We look at our errors and attempt to correct them. We experience the prewriting, drafting, revising, proofreading, and editing phases of the writing process with each other, supporting one another's understanding of what it means to write well. We have many opportunities to think about sequencing ideas, adding supporting details, structuring the flow of ideas and of sentences. We experience ways to go about editing our pieces as we look for "better" or "stronger" words. We begin taking steps in managing the mechanics and structures of writing. Our writing has a purpose—we want to tell a story. We are the "experts" who know this story. We have something to tell, and we are working together to find good ways to tell it. This group experience supports the individual students as they attempt to implement the writing process on their own.

On each story I include the words, "Written and Illustrated by . . ." with the name of the class or individuals in the group, the school, and the date. By giving attention to the authors and illustrators of the story, I find that the children have more of an investment in it. This, in turn, promotes reading because they have involved themselves in the entire story (see Figure 2).

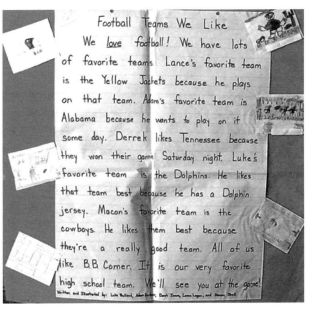

Figure 2. Typical large-group story displayed on classroom window shade (top); typical small-group story written by group of friends who enjoy football (right)

By keeping the illustrations small, all of them may be glued on or around the story, which I paste onto a large piece of colorful bulletin board paper for display. I encourage children to fill all the space on their illustration sheets and to make them as colorful as possible. I remind them to write their names on the back of their drawings so we will know whose name to give as illustrator under their picture.

In order to provide a quick, handy reference for busy teachers, I have condensed the previous discussion of creating whole-group and small-group stories based on children's interests (which can be found in Appendix D, "Nutshell" versions).

BIG BOOKS

One of the simplest class projects to make is a class big book. There are many options for doing this. You may wish to start early in the year with half-sheets of poster board or large construction paper, writing one line of a well-loved poem on each piece, and having children volunteer to act as illustrators for each page. Shel Silverstein's (1974) poem "Sick" works well for this.

Another type of big book might be a parallel story based on the children's favorite book. *If You Give a Mouse a Cookie*, by Laura Joffe Numeroff (1985), is an easy-to-use source for a parallel story. Have the children think of a character for their class book. Use large construction paper (at least 11" x 14") to form the pages of the book. Act as a scribe for the children, writing one sentence on each page, and let them choose which page they wish to illustrate. (Be sure to include enough episodes in the story so that each child will have his/her own page. Note the name of the illustrator under each picture.)

A different type of big book might evolve from a trip or experience that the class has had as a whole (see Elsewhere Expeditions in Chapter 5). For example, take the children out to collect insects. Have them make notes about what they did and what they found. Ask class members to dictate a story about the experience. Let them include photographs of the outing as well as drawings of the insects they found.

Another option is to take them to the school lunchroom for a behind-the-scenes tour and then have them dictate a group story about their experience. Include photographs of the tour and the children's drawings of what was most impressive to them. This outing is a good motivator for getting children to write because they are always amazed by the size of everything needed to prepare meals for large numbers of people.

Big books are very versatile and give the teacher an opportunity to guide children in organizing ideas, sequencing, mechanics, grammar, and other concepts (see Figure 3).

Figure 3. Example of whole-group big book following group inquiry session about "Jack and the Beanstalk"

Advantages of Making Class Big Books:

- Large size provides easy viewing by everyone.

- Format as whole-class project keeps students engaged in whole-part-whole strategy of literacy learning, especially if creating a parallel text. (Begin with whole text, break away to think about specific skill, embed that skill within the whole new text you are creating as a group.)

- Versatility of format lends itself to any genre and any grade level.

Examples of Skills Emphasized:

- Big books help children stay on a given topic.

- Big books encourage matching illustrations to text.

- The format can aid in sequencing ideas.

- Big books provide a way to focus on characters, setting, problem, solution, etc.

- Big books can address agreement of subject and verb.

- The format allows dialogue to be included within a text.

- Students can learn to include captions and labels in nonfiction big books.

BOUND BOOKS

Bound books are books that have been written by individuals or the class. Because I do many whole-group writings in other formats, I like to save the bound books for individually written projects that have been through all stages of the writing process and are ready to be published in a conventionally correct form.

The simplest way to bind books is to make the front and back covers from poster board or cardboard, use a hole punch to make one or more holes, and then insert rings, string, ribbon, or shoestrings as the binding.

If a bookbinding machine is available in the school, that is a wonderful way to keep children's writings in a permanent form. Although the machine itself is relatively expensive, one might be purchased for use by the entire school with general school funds or with funds from a grant. The binding combs are comparatively inexpensive and within the purchasing power of individual classrooms.

Binding books in hard covers can be a time-consuming process, so I call in parent or high school volunteers to help with this. Book covers can be made of cardboard or poster board covered with fabric, wallpaper, Con-Tact paper, or other such material. Place the cardboard (large enough to fold over and cover the book pages) flat and cover it with the material of choice. Stitch the book pages together by hand or machine, using long stitches, or staple them with a long-neck stapler. Place the assembled book pages inside the cover, spread glue over the inside of the front and back covers, and press the first and last pages of the book over the glued surfaces, smoothing firmly to remove any bubbles or wrinkles. (See Appendix E for detailed instructions on binding books with Con-Tact paper covers.)

Advantages of Using Bound Books:

- Relatively permanent binding keeps books in good repair for long periods of time.

- Format as an individual project engages students in whole-part-whole strategy of literacy learning.

- Versatility of format lends itself to any genre and any grade level.

Examples of Skills Emphasized:

- Bound books can stress writing to stay on a given topic.

- Bound books are good for matching illustrations to text.

- Bound books help in sequencing ideas.

- The format encourages attending to characters, setting, problem, solution, etc.

- Bound books can be focused on telling a story or explaining an event.

- The format allows inclusion of many details to enhance story line.

- The format provides an opportunity to include charts, diagrams, captions, and labels in nonfiction bound books.

BARE BOOKS

Bare books, available as hardcover or softcover, are pre-bound with blank pages. They offer a variety of cover designs and allow children to have permanently bound books without the teacher spending hours constructing them. Children love having their work published in these "real" books. They are produced by Treetop Publishing and may be purchased at a minimal cost through schools. By sending in a combined order, schools would be able to lower the cost per book. (See Appendix B for purchasing information.)

Advantages of Using Bare Books:

- Permanent binding preserves children's writing over a long period of time.

- Appearance of a "real book" is motivating to both reluctant and proficient writers.

- Versatility of format lends itself to any genre and any grade level.

- Format allows children to produce a final, polished version of a text without time-intensive binding preparation.

Examples of Skills Emphasized:

- Format encourages children to focus on appearance and mechanics after attending to content of a piece.

- Format is a vehicle for displaying child-created poetry, stories, chapter books, science experiments, etc.

- Children can easily insert photographs into this sturdy format to enhance autobiographies.

Bi-fold Books

Bi-fold books are a good alternative to hardcover books. Consisting of four or five sheets of 8 ½" x 11" blank white paper (such as photocopier paper), these simple books work well for young children and for most writing projects. Fold the pages in half crosswise and use a stapler to secure each book in three places along the fold. Children may want to add a construction paper cover when they have completed their books, or use the first page of the white paper as their cover, decorating it as desired (see Figure 4, page 54).

Advantages of Using Bi-fold Books:

- Bi-fold books are quickly and easily assembled.

- Easy format lends itself to volunteer or student preparation.

- Simple but versatile format allows multiple uses.

- Format is especially good for rough drafts of picture books (pages are easily cut, rearranged, and re-stapled).

- Format is adaptable to all genres and age levels.

- Format prevents misplacing draft pages.

- Bi-fold books are inexpensive to make.

- Books can be made as long or as short as the writer desires by adding or removing pages.

Examples of Skills Emphasized:

- Children can practice sequencing of events.

- Children can attend to descriptive details.

- Format encourages attention to conventions of language.

- This is a good retelling format: long enough, but not too long.

- This is a good format for writing plays or poetry.

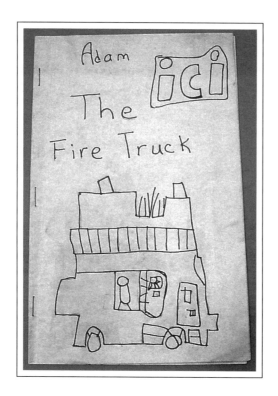

Figure 4. *Example of a bi-fold book*

ORGANIZATIONAL HINT:

Making bi-fold books is something with which I can always use help; and since I can explain how they are made in a matter of minutes, they make great jobs for parents, students from upper grades, or other volunteers. I ask the helpers to count out four or five pieces of paper, fold them in half, and staple along the fold in three places. Then they count the books into stacks of 25 and put a rubber band around each batch, placing them on the shelf for our use as needed. I can glance at the shelf the day before I want to use bi-fold books to see if our supply is adequate for the next day and quickly replenish it if necessary.

STEP BOOKS

Step books are made from three sheets of white paper (again, photocopier paper works well). Stagger the sheets so that each one is approximately 1¼ " above the bottom edge of the sheet below it. Then, holding the sheets in this position, fold all three sheets over so that the top portion is also spaced in the same manner. (This makes the top flap about 2¼" wide.) Staple along the fold. Now you have an 8½" x 8½" book consisting of six "steps," which may be used in a variety of ways.

Across the top flap the children might write the title and author of a book they have read and use the subsequent stepped pages to write about characters, setting, beginning, middle, and end—or characters, setting, problem, and solution—or to show the sequence of events in the story. I often have the students write on the part of the page that shows and draw illustrations on the part that is covered by the previous page, though it would also work the other way as well.

There are as many ways to use this versatile book design as there are teachers and children. Here's one example. On the first day of school, I have the children make a step book about themselves and include a photo at the end. They put their name at the top and use subsequent steps to tell about their family, their pets, their favorite things, their least favorite things, something they do well, something they wish they could do well, etc. This always creates enthusiasm for writing on that very important first day. We then mount these books on a bulletin board so that the children and I can learn more about each other. (See Appendix F for an example of a step book and construction directions.)

Advantages of Using Step Books:

- Short format is less intimidating to reluctant writers. (Most feel that they *can* write a title and five brief statements.)

- For students who have trouble knowing how to begin writing, the "steps" are often more manageable than long blank pages.

- By asking students to include an illustration under the flap and text on the part of the step that shows—or vice versa—reluctant writers can begin with the pictures so that they have "something to write about."

(continued)

- Versatile format lends itself easily to any genre and any grade level.

- This is a good report format for a book read, research conducted, etc.

Examples of Skills Emphasized:

- Step books are good for writing step-by-step depictions of science experiments.

- Format is good for step-by-step explanations of math problems.

- Step-by-step format makes logical sequencing easier for many students.

- This is a logical format for brief story summaries:

  - title/author, setting, characters, beginning, middle, and ending events

  - title/author, setting, characters, problem, resolution, time line of main events

- This is a good format for an "All About Me" book for the first day of school (my name, my address, my family, something I can do well, my favorite things, my picture on the first day of school).

FLIP BOOKS

Flip books provide another easy-to-make, versatile format for writing with young children. Simply take a sheet of 8 ½" x 11" white photocopier paper and fold it in half lengthwise so it measures 4 ¼" x 11". Cut the front only (up to the fold) at 2 ¾", 5 ½", and 8 ¼" intervals to form four separate flaps. (I usually stack a few sheets of paper together, fold them lengthwise, and cut through several thicknesses at a time, quickly producing enough books for my class in a preparation time of only two or three minutes.)

These books are one of my favorite formats for gaining a quick view of a child's grasp of a story, a book, an event, or an academic subject matter concept. I ask the children to write their name and title on the back. Then they might label their flaps (making illustrations or writing descriptions under the flap): "Characters," "Setting," "Problem," "Solution"; or "First," "Next," "Next," "Last"; or I might have students write a fact about a particular topic on each flap and illustrate it below. For a science experiment when we were forming crystals, I asked the children to draw what they saw in the microscope at hourly intervals and to write the time and a description of that stage of the experiment. After we had explored liquid measurement for some time, I asked my students to draw four different quantities that were equivalent on the front of the flaps and to tell inside how they might use those particular volume measures. My children often used this format independently as they chose to write up their projects or to make advertisements for books they had read. (See Appendix G for an example of a flip book and construction directions.)

Advantages of Using Flip Books:

- Short format is less intimidating to reluctant writers. (Most feel that they *can* write a title on the back and four brief statements.)

- For students who have trouble knowing how to begin writing, the "flaps" are more manageable than long blank pages.

- By asking students to include an illustration under the flap and text on the portion of the flap that shows—or vice versa—reluctant writers can begin with the pictures so that they have "some thing to write about."

- Step-by-step format makes logical sequencing easier for many students.

- Versatile format lends itself easily to any genre and any grade level.

Examples of Skills Emphasized:

- Brief story summaries are structured yet simple (title and author on back, beginning, middle, middle, end on front—or characters, setting, problem, solution).

- One-to-one matching of equivalent measurements allows room for math statement on flap and illustration under flap—or vice versa.

- Format allows for periodic recording of information over time (stages of growth of a bean sprout over two weeks' time, stages of crystal formation at hourly intervals, description and illustration of life cycle of a frog or other animal, variations in trees over the four seasons, etc.).

- Format allows child to structure a retelling to include pertinent information in a very brief way.

(continued)

- Format allows child to record four (or eight) important facts gained from a reading or an experiment. (I prefer four facts—with illustrations—for young children.)

JOURNALS

There are many ways to use journals with young children. I use them as a personal communication between the students and me and, thus, allow the children to determine what they write about. I treat these as "response journals," in that I respond to them by writing back.

At the beginning of the year I have students write in their journals every day, on whatever topics they choose—usually their pets, family, friends, trips, or play experiences. By suggesting that they write about something they want me to know about their lives, I give them the opportunity to "talk" to me on paper, rather than "stampede" to me as they walk in the door of the classroom. Now if they want to tell me about some person, activity, or event, they can write to me about it. I believe that one reason they continue to do this is because I take the time to write back to them. As the year progresses, I usually get into a pattern of having them write in journals on Mondays, Wednesdays, and Fridays for a specified period of time. Since I have required more writing of other types, it has worked well to have the journals cut to half-page size. This is less intimidating for the students and makes my job of responding to them less time-consuming. (I can usually respond to almost all during a 30-minute block, such as the time they are at P.E.)

In my classroom, journals are personal writings that are not shared (unless the child requests to do so). I begin by responding to each entry but usually cannot keep up with this for more than a week or two at the beginning of the year. After that, I respond to at least one entry per week. I use the journal to model correct spelling, grammar, punctuation, etc., as I include correct versions of most misspelled words in my response to the students. I feel that personal journal entries should not be corrected; however, it is quite appropriate to write back to the child, modeling conventions of spelling, grammar, etc. I write directly on the front of the child's entry if there is room so that the conventionally spelled words in my response are juxtaposed beside the original writing of the child. If there is not enough room for my response, I turn the page over and write on the back. This procedure has worked well for me over the many years I have used it.

I personally like using the response journal format to informally teach friendly-letter format in an authentic context. I simply answer each child's journal entry in friendly-letter format (which is a skill required for second graders in my district). Every year I am amazed at how quickly many students begin writing back to me in that same format—without any formal instruction in the technique. This informal, authentic practice sets the stage for later formal mini-lessons in which I directly teach friendly-letter format following our first class trip—which is usually an Elsewhere Expedition to the school lunchroom early in the fall semester. (See Chapter 5 for information about Elsewhere Expeditions.)

I like the personal response format because it helps me get to know the students, quickly informs me of their strengths and weaknesses in writing, and gives the students an opportunity to feel that I have personally spoken with each of them as they read my responses. Children rush to get their journals and eagerly read the responses. I do not have to coax them to write if I respond to them regularly and, by not having their writing directly corrected in this informal first-draft format, the students seem to write more than they otherwise might. My modeling of correct spelling and usage in the responses to student journaling is effective as a source to which students turn for later spelling references in their writing—both in their journaling and in their other types of writings. (See Appendix H for construction directions for half-page journals, an example of a student's journal, and one of my anecdotal record pages used at the very beginning of the year.)

ORGANIZATIONAL HINT:

I store journals and logs, folded back to the last entry, in clear plastic shoeboxes so that I can easily and quickly find the page to which I need to respond. I also make sure that each type of log is covered in a different color of construction paper (e.g., journals are blue, science logs are orange, math logs are red, reading logs are green, etc.). This helps the students (and me) keep separate the different formats for writing and easily locate the different types as we need them. (I usually make these journals 20 half-sheet pages long. When the first journal is completed, the child gets journal #2, #3, etc. Children often express a sense of accomplishment as they move from one journal to the next.)

I try to stay ahead in making the journals, storing those in process and those completed in separate stacks on a shelf. Classroom volunteers, my students who have extra time, or older students who come in to help may count out pages, stacking them crosswise in groups of 10 sheets. Then, when an adult has time to cut them in half with the paper cutter, those cut halves may be stacked crosswise in double sets (20 pages in each set) for later binding. Construction paper covers are made in sufficient quantities for each type of journal being prepared—for example, 50 red halves will prepare 25 journals (front and back covers for each). Then, when there is time to bind the journals, it is not a time-consuming task.

Advantages of Using Journals:

- Response journals allow children choice in revealing personal information that they want the teacher to have about them.

- Response journals build personal relationships between teachers and children in a nonthreatening way.

- Journals allow children to write as "experts" about a topic they know well.

- Half-page journal size is less intimidating to students and less time-intensive for teachers as they respond.

- Journaling allows children and teachers (and parents, if the child agrees) to see growth in children's writing across time.

Examples of Skills Emphasized:

- Journals are a good place to talk to children about sticking to a topic and giving many details about that topic.

- For response journals I usually *model* correct sentence structure, spelling, subject/verb agreement, etc., in my response to the child, rather than correct the child's own words.

- Journals are an easy way to introduce friendly-letter format. (I respond to the journals in this format most of the time.)

Writing Logs

Writing logs are similar to journals but may be used in a variety of ways for a variety of subjects. Journals are a place for my students to write on a free choice of subject in whatever format they choose. Writing logs are somewhat more structured in that children respond to assigned questions or topics, although there is still a large element of choice in how they answer the prompts they are given.

For very young children I make short logs by binding approximately 20 half-page sheets of 8½" x 11" paper per log. I use construction paper for the covers, with a different color for each type of log. As children come into the class and wait for others to arrive, I sometimes have them write in their logs, usually a math log one day, a logic log (see next page) on another, and so forth. I use journal writing, however, as a reflective close to an activity or to end the day.

Math Logs

Half-page math logs are used for working a daily word problem. I put a word problem on the board (usually a little in advance of whatever we are studying in class) so that the children have to use their ingenuity to solve it. I ask them to write the word problem, solve it with pictures or numbers, and tell in words how they solved it or why they solved it in the way that they did. They can usually do the entire process using the front and the back of a page. When all of the children have completed their math logs, I ask someone to go to the board to show his/her solution. Then we look for others who have solved the problem in a different way. I think it is very important to have children look for multiple solutions to problems. This has been a worthwhile process for the students and becomes easier as the year progresses.

(For ease of management, these have covers of a different color from those of journals and other logs, and they are stored in clear plastic shoeboxes with the logs folded back to the last problem so that I can easily and quickly glance through them. I do not grade these logs, but I do check to see if they are done and if someone has obvious confusion.)

Logic Logs

I encourage children to work in their logic logs once a week or at least every other week. I write a simple logic problem on the board for the students to write in their logic logs and try to solve as they first enter the class. Their assignment is to write the problem, solve it, and tell in words how they solved it. We share solutions when all children have attempted to solve it. Children become better at understanding how to go about solving logic problems as they gain experience with them. Again, these half-page logs have construction paper covers of a color different from that of other logs and journals.

A good source of logic problems is *Mind Benders: Deductive Thinking Skills*, by Harnadek (1978), published by Critical Thinking Books & Software. This company publishes logic problems suitable for kindergartners through adults. (See Appendix B for web site and contact information for obtaining a catalog.)

"Think About" Logs

"Think About" Logs are half-page journals in which the students write about a particular topic. I ask them to stop what they are doing and think about the topic we have been discussing or studying—or one that we are ready to begin studying—and to briefly record their ideas on paper. This is a first-draft form of writing that allows them to capture their thoughts before sharing them aloud with the group. It forces all of the students to concentrate on the topic and not just rely on one or two of their more vocal classmates to speak for them. It serves as an anecdotal record of their thinking that allows me to identify misconceptions and to point out growth over time to students, parents, administrators, and other interested individuals. Entries in this log are dated, as are entries in other journals and logs.

Reading Logs

Reading log assignments might consist of a story summary or a written retelling, including descriptions of the character, setting, problem, solution; beginning, middle, end; favorite part; author and/or illustrator studies; etc. These logs are particularly suited to spiral notebooks because:

1) The children can keep their entries in order.

2) They can fold back their entries so I can easily find them for grading.

3) I can fold them back so they can easily read my most recent comment to them.

4) The progression of their work and writing over time is available to the child, to parents, and to me as we conference about the child's reading.

I do not have children write in reading logs every day, but they are frequently given assignments to write in their reading logs. In one section of the log I ask the students to keep a list of the books they have read. At the beginning of the year I sometimes staple lists of available books to the inside cover of the notebook (or to folders) and have students check off what they have read. As they become more proficient writers and readers, I turn that duty over to them entirely.

Science Logs

Science logs also lend themselves to spiral notebooks for the same reasons mentioned in reading logs. Additionally, since these notebooks lie flat, putting notes on one page and additional commentary and/or illustrations on the opposite page allows more in-depth information to be recorded in a format that keeps the two pages connected and that is easily located. Children take their science logs with them on science expeditions to make notes, draw pictures of things they have found, record observations, make lists of characteristics, etc.

Science logs are for first-draft writing. They are a good place to keep notes when looking up information in an area of science and to record questions that they would like to explore in future investigations. Nancie Atwell's (1990) *Coming to Know: Writing to Learn in the Middle Grades* includes wonderful ways to use science logs. Although her text is written for older students, many of the ideas have worked well in both my first- and second-grade classes.

There are countless ways to use writing logs in all subject areas. Try them in your classroom to discover those that work best for you and your students. The important thing is to have the students reading, observing, questioning, thinking, and expressing their ideas in written form for reflection.

Advantages of Using Writing Logs:

- Writing logs allow children choices in responding to various content and topics.

- Writing logs build personal relationships between teachers and children in a nonthreatening way.

- Half-page-size logs are less intimidating to students and less time-intensive for teachers as they respond.

- Writing in content area logs allows children, teachers, and parents to see growth in children's writing across time.

Examples of Skills Emphasized:

- **Math logs** lend themselves to having children write word problems, solve them with numbers, and then explain in words how or why they solved the problem in that way. Other skills in math include measurement, temperature, ordinals, charting, and graphing.

- **Logic logs** are a place for children to write logic problems, solve them, and then tell how and why they solved them as they did.

- **"Think About" logs** allow children to reflect about the day's events, a topic we have been discussing or studying, problems we are experiencing in our classroom, etc.

- **Reading logs** give children a place to record information about books they have read, authors they are studying, etc. Book summaries, reflections on specific aspects of a book, and Venn diagrams comparing/contrasting two books the child has read are some of the ways reading logs are used in my class.

- **Science logs** are used to record notes from our observations or experiments, to keep questions that they would like to explore in future investigations, to take notes from readings, to brainstorm questions and find answers, and to reflect about particular science topics as we study them. (See Figure 10, page 106, for examples from one child's science log.)

A True "Cautionary Tale"— with a Happy Ending

It *is* possible to overuse logs and journaling, thereby turning children against writing altogether. I do suggest, however, giving students real purposes for their writing and in as many ways as are practical. By varying the formats, times, and purposes of writing, children will become thinkers who have an "author mindset." A perfect example of this comes to mind:

It had become almost a joke between my second-grade students and me that I would make them write about whatever we were doing, and one spring, I experienced a classroom revolt! Our school was anticipating the arrival of an outstanding children's theater group from a nearby urban area. They were scheduled to come to our school gymnasium and perform a play based upon a well-known children's story. Teachers were collecting one dollar from each student who could afford to pay—but none of *my* students brought in their money. I was amazed that they did not want to attend and I said to them, "This play will be wonderful. The story is exciting; the costumes and props will be unbelievable. Why don't you want to go to see it?" Their response came quickly, "You'll just make us *write* about it!" I pointed to myself and asked innocently, "Me?" They all laughed. I said, "Well, I'll make you a deal. If you go, I won't make you write about it." They looked dubious and said, "You promise?" I said, "I promise." In the next few days their dollars began trickling in until all had paid.

The day of the performance came. As I was leading my line of "ducklings" back to our classroom following the exciting performance, I heard one bold voice pipe up behind me, "Mrs. Stewart, do you remember what you promised?"

I turned to Jessica, genuinely puzzled, and asked, "What are you talking about?" She stopped, propped her hands on her hips, and said, "You know . . . you *promised* we wouldn't have to write about that play!" I grinned at her and said casually, "Yeah. I remember . . . you don't have to write about it." She said, "Good. But if I *did* have to write about it I'd say . . .," and she began telling a remarkable version of the story we had just enjoyed together.

Her retelling lasted throughout the entire walk back to our classroom—which was all the way across the campus from the gym! I was very excited. *This* was exactly what I wanted for my students—to have them so internalize their sense of authorship that every experience was viewed from an author's perspective.

WRITING FROM LITERATURE

Chapter 4

Writing from literature is one of my favorite ways of writing with children, and it is easy to build on my own enthusiasm. Every day I share books that I like. Young children can be guided into enjoyment of many types of literature, and I always try to remember that, as the teacher, it is *my* response that is contagious. If I love a book or poem and obviously enjoy sharing it, there is a greater likelihood that the children will experience those same reactions. They often request particular pieces over and over (just like many children at home do for their favorite bedtime stories). It is not only the special story, but also the good feeling accompanying it, as well as the connection with the teacher, that the students seem to crave.

The wealth of good literature available to us to use with children is a wonderful springboard into a variety of types of writing. As I have said earlier, I feel it is important to help children see the interconnectedness of reading and writing. I believe this for many reasons, but primarily because children who perceive themselves as authors are empowered in every area of the language arts.

ORGANIZATIONAL HINTS:

Gather the children around you so that they anticipate hearing a good story. Peterson (1992) likens this to the opening curtain of a play. I like to think of it as another way of opening the drawstring bag, preparing the audience (in this case, the children) to explore the world of stories. This is the same procedure I use when conducting mini-lessons. As I described in Chapter 2, this brings them physically close to me, and also enables me to catch a student's attention if he or she becomes distracted or begins to disturb other listeners. Sometimes my simply stopping and looking at the individuals who are behaving inappropriately during a story refocuses their attention and allows me to continue without verbally interrupting the flow of the story.

Not only is the gathering of children a

(continued)

good classroom organizational strategy, but so is the structuring of the classroom environment. For example, I arrange the desks so they encircle a large open area that contains an area rug on which the children sit for group times and when they are working independently, with partners, or in small groups. The simple act of calling the children as a group to the rug is an organizational strategy that quickly lets them know they are expected to gather, to participate in a group activity, and to be an attentive audience for whoever is sharing his or her ideas, comments, stories, or lessons.

I place large pillows, beanbags (some that I purchased at yard sales and others that children brought from home), or other comfortable seating around the outer border of our rug. This allows me to point to students who are really listening and participating so that they can quietly move to those more relaxed places. (I always leave at least one pillow vacant until very near the end of our group time so that all children continue to feel that they have an opportunity to sit there.)

Another organizational strategy is the use of the author's chair. A full discussion of this may be found in "The Author's Chair" (Hansen and Graves 1983). In our classroom, when a student is sitting in the author's chair, all of us anticipate hearing a story from that child. We know what the rules are during this time: listening quietly as the piece is read, thinking intently about questions we have for the author, taking turns asking our questions (or answering questions from the author), and preparing to give constructive feedback to tell the author what additional information we need as readers and listeners.

One final organizational strategy is the arrangement of the print-rich environment described in Chapter 2. Necessary books, supplies, equipment, and information are placed so that students can easily access what they need without disturbing others who are working. Shelves and card racks are arranged along two walls, facing the open areas of the classroom. Multiple sets of supplies are available in work stations around the classroom. Cabinets are labeled and available to students for general supplies. Word walls are located so that students can see them easily and arranged so that words are readily accessible: some listed under letters of the alphabet, some in groups such as names, holidays, etc., some in word families we have studied.

Everything in the environment works toward making our literacy lives together productive, easy, calm, and inviting—a place where a community of co-learners is working and spending time together—a place where everyone belongs, knows what to do, and can efficiently find what is needed.

Once the children are familiar with the structure and procedures of the classroom, being productive becomes much easier. In this chapter, I invite you to think about using many kinds of literature to encourage your students to be engaged and active learners. I discuss a particular literature focus, followed by annotated examples of literature that have been successful in my classrooms. These sources are helpful to children as they listen to and learn from the language of story; as they struggle to construct their own versions of other authors' stories; as they create their own original tales; and as they learn about the content, structure, and conventions of writing by examining in detail the work of other authors. I begin with my favorite format of literature—picture books.

USING PICTURE BOOKS TO SPARK IDEAS

I use simple picture books in which illustrations expand the text to introduce children to creating their own picture books. With my very young learners I show them many excellent examples of these books in which only one sentence is written on each page, and this is the format that I encourage them to use at the beginning. I point out expressions on the faces of characters and the importance of using illustration details to expand the meaning of the text. I take time to read several good picture books to the children, pointing out the placement of pictures and text on the page. I have them note that sometimes text is above the illustration, sometimes beside or below it; sometimes one page may contain text only, with illustrations on the facing page. I tell them that placement of picture and text on the page is a matter of personal choice. We talk about the techniques the author uses in the first few pages of the book to "open his or her story" and on the last few pages to "draw it to a close" (like opening and closing a drawstring bag).

Reading picture books to children is a very easy way to get across to them the concept of staying on the subject when writing. They quickly see that in published books the pictures go exactly with the text and that all of the ideas connect to a central theme. By taking time to point this out to them and to discuss examples in various books, I am able to teach the children how to incorporate those features in their own picture book creations. They learn to write one sentence per page and illustrate only that one statement. Then they learn to read their pages in the order they have written them, thinking about how the ideas connect to the overall theme of their book. This practice allows off-the-subject sentences and ideas to stand out as inappropriate in their own versions of picture books. Because staying on topic is one of the most difficult concepts to get across to young writers, it is effective to have children create picture books often at the beginning of the school year. As children graduate from writing picture books to other genres of writing, most retain the idea that they must stick to a topic.

Creating picture books also gives the advantage of flexibility to children. Each page consists of one sentence with an accompanying illustration. If a child gets the sequence of his/her story somewhat confused or out of order—or if more elaboration is needed—it is an easy task to rearrange, add, or remove pages. My students find it helpful to pencil in a tentative page number on the back of each first-draft page of their picture books. Then, after they have finished revising, proofreading, and editing, they put the final page number on the front of each page. The ability to move pages around saves a great deal of rewriting—which is particularly important to children for whom writing is literally a struggle. Use of this simple, flexible format makes writing stories "child-friendly" and seems to promote a good attitude as children approach the task. They do not seem to mind my suggesting that they "redo" their stories to improve on the sequence or to "add a page to tell more about. . . ."

I can recall a particular instance in which a bright young second grader had written a lengthy story about a football game, filling every line on the front and back of his pages. Right in the middle of that story he had a sentence about getting a new baby brother at his house. The sentence had no connection with his story. When I conferenced with him about his story and suggested that he omit that sentence from his football story and possibly write another story about his new baby brother, he cried, saying that he didn't want to have to write that whole story again. If I had been using the picture book format at the time, this stressful situation could have been avoided. He would have been able to remove that page about his brother and save it for his next picture book. It was that unfortunate incident that prompted me to change the way I began writing with young children.

Advantages of Using Picture Books for Writing:

- Picture books seem to be the easiest format to use in the beginning stages of writing to help children stay on the subject.

- They help children attend to one aspect of a story at a time.

- Once the ideas are on separate pages, the flexible picture book format allows children to contemplate the sequence and logical flow of ideas and to easily rearrange pages as necessary.

- Children can proofread and edit with confidence, knowing that they will need to correct only those particular pages with specific corrections.

- Picture books allow children's artistic talents to be displayed as they create illustrations for their books.

- Picture books are a "showy" format that allows children—as well as their peers and parents—to see their efforts in an impressive finished product.

Creating carefully prepared picture books helps children realize that they have created a "real" book and that they are "real" authors. They appear much more interested in details of picture books created by other authors and illustrators once they have experienced the process themselves and usually begin attempting in their own books some of the more sophisticated strategies used by professional authors and illustrators. Picture books—especially picture storybooks, which convey their message through illustration and the written word—are really a *format* of writing rather than a *genre* of literature. The format refers to the structure of the book, which is usually relatively uncomplicated text (though not always on simplistic subjects) accompanied by illustrations that range from simple to quite complex. Genre refers to the type or style of book, such as autobiography, biography, tall tales, folktales, poetry, nonfiction, etc. Books of many genres appear in picture book format. One aspect of picture books that seems key is that the text and the illustrations are intricately coordinated. It is by reading and closely examining outstanding picture books that children easily learn to pay attention to both the art of writing and the art of illustration in their own picture book creations.

ORGANIZATIONAL HINT:

When very young children are just beginning to create picture books, it is helpful to have each of them make one page for a class picture book. The children's individual pages are then bound together for the class book, which may be checked out and shared through the class library. Alternatively, copies may be duplicated for each child. After making several jointly composed class books, the students will require less one-on-one instruction in the process of formatting their individual picture books, though they will continue to need instruction in the processes of prewriting, drafting, revising, proofreading, and editing.

With very young children, the first few picture books need not always be edited or displayed. The books of children who are willing to share them should be read to the class by the student or the teacher (whichever the child prefers), having the teacher point out the "good things" about that book to the author in a very enthusiastic manner. This helps all of the children realize that writing is a personally rewarding, nonthreatening experience. Almost immediately those same "good things" will turn up in the writing of other class authors.

"Good things" that might be in a student's book:

- Stayed on the subject and "made sense."

- Had strong ideas and an interesting story line.

- Contained many details to help the reader/listener understand the story.

- Had pictures that illustrated the accompanying text.

- Used good, strong vocabulary even if not spelled in a conventionally correct manner.

- Contained the word "I," written as a capital letter.

- Contained sentences that started with a capital and ended with a period (or question mark or exclamation point).

- Contained dialogue (at which point quotation marks might be explained).
- Contained sentences in which the author put the other person first ("Mommy and I played ball," etc., rather than "Me and daddy cooked dinner," which is the typical word order used by young children).

Explicitly pointing out these good things when they occur helps children recognize them in their own work and strive to incorporate them more often. When I say to students, "Wow! You just did something really smart! Can you tell me what you did that was so good?", they will name some of these "good things," letting me see that they have internalized a recognition of those elements as desirable in their writing.

LITERATURE EXAMPLES:

Golly Gump Swallowed a Fly
by Joanna Cole (1981), illustrated by Bari Weisman

Golly Gump Swallowed a Fly is especially good for explaining the picture book format to young children. Weisman creates illustrations that use exaggerated expressions and an expanding stomach for Golly Gump, which immediately capture the attention of young readers/authors. They readily understand the importance of letting the pictures reflect the words of their stories after exploring the relationship of illustration and text in this book. The delightful absurdity of this story is highly appropriate for young readers/writers.

Rainbow Fish
written and illustrated by Marcus Pfister (1992)

This gorgeous picture book shows children the power of illustrations. The idea of sharing is dramatically brought forward through text and illustrations. Children enjoy retelling this story and then using a turquoise watercolor wash together with glitter or sequins to make their own version of the Rainbow Fish tale (see Figure 5). For specific painting directions, see "Activity" on pages 90–91. This Swedish text is an excellent example of a translated picture book that presents the opportunity to talk with children about various techniques used by authors of different cultures. A good picture book to contrast with other cultural techniques is *I'm in Charge of Celebrations* by Byrd Baylor (1986), discussed on page 83.

Figure 5. Follow-up rainbow fish project using crayon-resist art technique, with glitter on scales and a blue bead "eye"

The Very Hungry Caterpillar
written and illustrated by Eric Carle (1981)

This delightful picture book shows children ways to illustrate their texts in a step-by-step manner. Its predictability makes it easy to pattern as a parallel story. It is especially good for showing large, almost page-size illustrations so children realize that pictures can carry the story as much as words. The large, vivid drawings help children understand the power of big pictures in their own stories. It is also an excellent book to use to point out building a story to a climax.

READING AND WRITING ABOUT FEELINGS

Sharing books with young readers is an excellent way to get them to think about feelings they have and to be able to express those feelings verbally and in writing. It is also a good way to teach children to consider the feelings of others. In addition, it helps to forge bonds of closeness in a classroom community as children come together to hear and respond to literature in a group setting. Follow-up voluntary sharings of their written responses can be a powerful way for children to show support of one another as they respond to what has been written and shared.

LITERATURE EXAMPLES:

The Patchwork Quilt
by Valerie Flournoy (1985), illustrated by Jerry Pinkney

One of my favorite books to share with children is *The Patchwork Quilt*. This is a touching story about a patchwork quilt being made by a young girl's grandmother, who becomes ill. The quilt is cut from scraps of the family's old clothes and tells the story of their lives. The warm feelings between the girl, Tanya, and her grandmother as the quilt is being made spark reminiscences from children about their own family experiences. This book makes a lovely starting place for writing about sharing and relationships between children and their family members, and is multicultural literature that is culturally appropriate, as are the following two examples.

Grandpa's Face
by Eloise Greenfield (1988), illustrated by Floyd Cooper

This story, dealing with love and trust between a young girl and her grandpa, sparks a wonderful discussion with children as to their own experiences with grandparents and other relatives. It is a good springboard for getting children to recall and write about their personal feelings about family members.

She Come Bringing Me That Little Baby Girl
by Eloise Greenfield (1974), illustrated by John Steptoe

This story of an older brother's feelings when a new baby enters his family helps children get in touch with their own feelings about changes in their families. By writing about those changes, children are often able to come to terms with them and find something positive about them.

Next Year I'll Be Special
by Patricia Reilly Giff (1980a), illustrated by Marylin Hafner

This is the story of a first grader who is unhappy with her teacher's way of doing things, and longs for the next year, when she will be in Miss Lark's second-grade class and be "special." The entire book is a future vision of ways the young student will be special in her new class. It provides children with ideas about how they can try to help others feel special and is a good starting place for writing about that.

Today Was a Terrible Day
by Patricia Reilly Giff (1980b), illustrated by Susanna Natti

Second grader Ronald Morgan suffers one mishap after another in Miss Tyler's class but finally realizes that he has a wonderful new ability—he can read! Children identify with how Ronald feels in each situation and are able to write about what it would feel like to be Ronald or how they might help him if they were his classmates. This book is rich with writing potential.

USING HUMOR TO CAPTURE THE IMAGINATION OF CHILDREN

Young children have a wonderfully absurd sense of the ridiculous, and they delight in books and stories that capture their silly side. Funny stories are quickly read and reread in classrooms of young learners. In fact, some of my favorite memories are of times when students were so

captivated by the humor in a poem or story that they rushed to read it to me, saying, "You've just gotta hear this!" Funny stories and poems may be used effectively to help children write their own silly creations. Children are very enthusiastic about creating humorous books of their own.

Literature Examples:

Amelia Bedelia
by Peggy Parrish (1963), illustrated by Fritz Siebel

This and other Amelia Bedelia books by Peggy Parrish tell the adventures of a zany character who is employed as a maid and takes every order from her employers at its literal meaning. Children love to hear story after story about Amelia Bedelia and her exploits. These books, rich with vocabulary which may be interpreted in more than one way, give teachers many opportunities to explore word meanings with their students in a very entertaining format. Children may choose to create their own Amelia Bedelia adventures or their own character who experiences misadventures through a play on words. As I read the Amelia Bedelia books to students, I always deliberately stop and have children predict the way Amelia Bedelia will interpret the instructions she receives—so that they are thinking of multiple meanings of words. This is an easy way to build facility with words.

The Stupids Die
by Harry Allard (1981), illustrated by James Marshall

The Stupids Have a Ball
by Harry Allard (1978), illustrated by James Marshall

The slapstick humor and ridiculous pictures in these two books capture the fancy of young children. Illustrations and text are combined in such a way that children literally rush to reread them. It is easy for children to get ideas from these books and write their own versions of the "Stupid" family or an opposite version of the "Smart" family. Both books lend themselves well to a small-group writing project in which several children work together to create a "Stupids" book (see Figure 6). Several children may choose to work as writers while others may be illustrators or color artists. One child may act as chairman of the group and help make decisions when necessary.

(**Note:** Remarkably, the term "Stupid" is applied only as a last name to the characters in the original book or the spin-offs and does not seem to enter into the classroom in other ways.)

Figure 6. Examples from student-written text to parallel Allard and Marshall's (1981) "Stupids" family

A Light in the Attic
written and illustrated by Shel Silverstein (1981)

Where the Sidewalk Ends
written and illustrated by Shel Silverstein (1974)

Shel Silverstein is very effective with young children because of the way he uses humor in poetry and pictures. Children who are exposed to his silly poems and illustrations hurry to share their "finds" with their friends. Boys, especially, are drawn to his particular brand of humor. These two—my favorites among Silverstein's works—are musts in every teacher's classroom. (Refer to the following section on poetry for specifics about these books.)

Exploring Poetry with Young Children

Young children who have poetry read to them develop an appreciation for that genre. As they realize that poetry does not always have to rhyme and that it is appropriate for a wide range of subject matter and styles, they easily see themselves as poets and enthusiastically create unique poems of their own.

Literature Examples:

A Light in the Attic
written and illustrated by Shel Silverstein (1981)

Where the Sidewalk Ends
written and illustrated by Shel Silverstein (1974)

These two books give children a different appreciation for poetry than they receive from other sources. Children often spontaneously compose their own poems after being immersed in Silverstein's work. Their imaginations are sparked by his "gross" pictures, the particular rhythm of his verse, the shape of his poems, the vivid mental images conjured up by his words, the sounds of his poetry, the range of subjects, and the wild freedom of thought these poems engender. My students quickly fell in love with "Smart" and "Sick" from *Where the Sidewalk Ends* (1974). They took turns acting out "Smart," as we were studying money in math. Before everyone had had a turn to participate, the class had memorized the entire poem (and they repeated it throughout that year!). They also learned "Sick" and made a class book of that poem in which each line was written on a separate page and illustrated by a different student (see Figure 7).

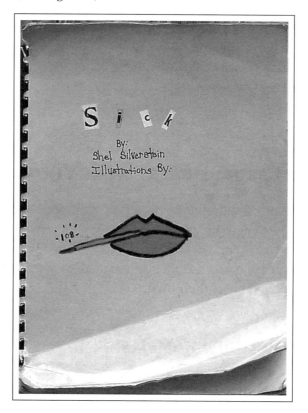

Figure 7. *Tattered and well-loved class version of Silverstein's (1974) "Sick," with illustrations by class members*

In addition to "Smart" and "Sick," other particular favorites for use with young children are Silverstein's (1974) "Lazy Jane," "Poem on the Neck of a Running Giraffe," and "Boa Constrictor," as well as "Twistable, Turnable Man," from his 1981 collection. Children may be encouraged to write their own versions of "Smart" and "Sick," to play with the shapes of their own poems (as in "Lazy Jane" and "Poem on the Neck of a Running Giraffe"), and to experiment with rhythm and patterns (as in

"Twistable, Turnable Man" and "Boa Constrictor"). Many other adaptations are possible based on Silverstein's poetry. His newer book of poems, *Falling Up* (1996), and his moving story about giving, *The Giving Tree* (1964), are also excellent additions for any early childhood classroom library.

Tickle Day: Poems from Father Goose
by Charles Ghigna (1994), illustrations by Cyd Moore

Charles Ghigna was invited to share his poetry with the Young Authors' Conference, which was held at our school several years ago. He told the children many stories about how he got ideas for his poetry. Because we were so fascinated with his tales, I purchased several volumes of his writing, my favorite among them being *Tickle Day: Poems from Father Goose*. Ghigna is very familiar with themes that appeal to young children, having based most of the poems in this book on the interests of his young son, Chip. "Little Daddy Longlegs" is a poem about a spider, inspired by an incident with a Granddaddy Longlegs that was climbing up his front porch steps. "On the Way to School" is a child's perfect excuse for being tardy to school, and "Turtle Trouble" is easily understood by any child who has attempted to coax a turtle out of its shell. Perhaps the one best loved by my very young students is "Tomorrow's My Birthday," as it speaks of what a child will do when he reaches the "great age" of four. These poems encourage children to write about their own experiences in poetic form. Finding a published writer who will come in and share his or her works and tell about how he/she created them is a wonderful way to help children gain confidence and ideas for their own writing.

"Honey, I Love," from *Honey, I Love and Other Love Poems*
by Eloise Greenfield (1972), illustrated by Diane and Leo Dillon

This heartwarming poem by Eloise Greenfield is a special one to share with children of any age, but particularly with young students as they begin learning about many types of literature. The good feelings engendered by this poem lend themselves to expression through child-created pictures, poetry, and stories based on the poem.

It is just as effective for use with boys as it is with girls. In fact, I firmly believe that it was the emotional pull and the comforting rhythm of this poem that enabled one of my young second graders to learn to read. He was a struggling reader when he discovered this poem in my student teacher's "big red notebook" of poetry that she shared with the class from time to time. He was a fetal-alcohol-syndrome baby who had many difficulties in addition to his problems with reading. But this child would go to her—and to me—again and again, pleading with us to read Greenfield's poem to him. We read it to him over and over. He gradually memorized it and was able to "read" it to himself and to other children.

From his love of this particular poem, he began exploring other poems available in the room. He seemed to believe that he was able to "read" the short stories captured in poetic form. He worked and worked and worked until he could read poem after poem.

The works of Eloise Greenfield and Shel Silverstein unlocked the reading process for him. Of this I have no doubt. The reader who struggled the most that year, he came back to me every year after he left my classroom to share his favorite stories and poems with the students in my succeeding classes. I always took time for him to do that—not only because I wanted to support his desire to read to others, but also because I thought that perhaps his enthusiasm for poetry would be contagious and capture the imagination of other young listeners and readers.

Read-Aloud Rhymes for the Very Young
selected by Jack Prelutsky (1986), illustrated by Marc Brown

This delightful collection of 200 poems is full of fun and energy for children of all ages. From Margaret Hillert's "Hide-and-Seek Shadow" to Evelyn Beyer's "Jump or Jiggle," children find catchy rhythms, inviting movements, and appealing pictures as they chant together words that engage them in language learning. Activities present themselves to teachers and students alike as they read Lenore M. Link's "Holding Hands" and Jack Pretlutsky's "Somersaults." Some of the poems, such as Dr. Seuss's "Quack, Quack!" and Mary Ann Hoberman's "Yellow Butter," have such compelling rhythms that children immediately respond by chanting the lines over and over. This book is essential to every classroom of young students. Children quickly become involved in the rhythms and illustrations and realize that they, too, can create poems and rhymes.

I'm in Charge of Celebrations
by Byrd Baylor (1986), illustrated by Peter Parnall

Baylor's picture storybook, set in the Southwest desert country, tells about some experiences that became her own special celebrations. This text, written in poetic prose, encourages children to write about their own special days that they want to remember. This is a great book to use in a poetry workshop because it shows prose written in the format of poetry. It inspires children to plan and describe their own celebrations. This good example of culturally appropriate multicultural literature helps children appreciate the specialness of nature and encourages them to take time to look for small wonders in the world around them. I particularly like to use this book in combination with others Baylor has written in partnership with illustrator Peter Parnall. Two other of my favorites follow. When multiple works by the same writers and artists are shared together, it helps children recognize the style of both author and illustrator.

Your Own Best Secret Place
by Byrd Baylor (1979), illustrated by Peter Parnall

This earlier work of the Baylor/Parnall team helps children think about the pleasures to be found in their own private places. This Native American author shares through her lyric prose a story describing how she found a hollow at the base of a cottonwood tree. Children can imagine her surprise when she discovered that it had been someone else's special place, too. The story—of her curling up warm and cozy inside the tree, contemplating her sense of sharing with the absent William Cottonwood, which leads her to describe other special places—helps children think about their own best secret spaces. After reading or hearing this story, children like to write about their favorite places. This book works especially well in combination with *I'm in Charge of Celebrations*.

The Table Where Rich People Sit
by Byrd Baylor (1994), illustrated by Peter Parnall

The third of my Baylor/Parnall favorites to share with children is this tale, also written in poetic prose. I particularly like it because of its theme. Mountain Girl calls a family meeting (held around the family's old homemade wooden table) to discuss the fact that her family isn't rich and to suggest what she thinks they need to do about it. She talks to them about their lack of money, but her father and mother share with her how rich they already are in the ways that matter, counting up the value of the special things in their lives. The story ends with Mountain Girl's realization that they *are* rich in the ways that count. As her family leaves to go outside and enjoy the new sliver of moon, she stays at the table to write, deciding to call her book *The Table Where Rich People Sit*. This book is particularly good at introducing Native American appreciation of nature and values. It also helps children realize how *they* are rich in important ways. I always follow this story by having children write their own version of *The Table Where Rich People Sit*.

All of Baylor's stories leave readers/listeners with an appreciation of special moments that no amount of money can buy. Parnall's unique illustrations enhance the specialness of Baylor's words as she shares her philosophy with readers of all ages. The team has received recognition for their collaborative work on three Caldecott Honor books: *The Way to Start a Day* (1978); *Hawk, I'm Your Brother* (1976); and *The Desert Is Theirs* (1975).

SHARING AUTOBIOGRAPHICAL STORIES THAT APPEAL TO YOUNG WRITERS

One of the most effective ways to encourage young writers to fill their stories with rich details and meaningful content is to have them write about their own experiences. (See Chapter 5 for ideas about helping children do this.) To show them that "real" authors do this also, it is important to share read-alouds with autobiographical content. (Read-alouds are books that are read aloud to children. In school settings, this is usually done as a whole-group activity. Trelease's [1995] work in the area of reading aloud to children stresses its importance, especially with regard to helping children become readers themselves; building a lifetime love of reading; supporting and extending spoken and written language; and improving vocabulary, spelling, and writing.) When possible, I always try to combine two books by the same author to give an expanded view of that author's style.

LITERATURE EXAMPLES:

Thunder Cake
written and illustrated by Patricia Polacco (1990)

This tale is based on the author's childhood experience in which her Russian grandma (her babushka) helped her lose her fear of thunderstorms. The counting sequences in the book appeal to young children as they help the young character count down the approaching thunderstorm. Children identify with the scary experiences the main character must endure in her attempt to prepare "Thunder Cake" with her grandmother. Almost every child has his or her own frightening recollections of thunderstorms to share in writing, and invariably some child will make "Thunder Cake" at home, following the recipe given at the end of the book, and bring it in to share with the class. This is another example of culturally appropriate multicultural literature.

My Rotten Redheaded Older Brother
written and illustrated by Patricia Polacco (1994)

Read as a follow-up to *Thunder Cake*, this true story, about the author and her older brother as they try to gain the advantage over each other, sends children into tale after tale of their own about siblings or cousins. The book, which includes photographs of the author and her brother as they grow and change over the years, intrigues children. They pore over the photos to get a sense of the author's real life. They enjoy comparing the illustrations to those in *Thunder Cake*, which also show young Tricia and her babushka. Children launch into stories about their own families and may easily be persuaded to write some of those stories for sharing with others. Any of Polacco's many books appeal to young writers and readers. Visit **http://www.patriciapolacco.com** for more information.

Memories: An Autobiography
by Mem Fox (1992)

This big book is filled with chapters containing photographs of the author at various stages of her life, as well as text telling of her growing-up years. Mem Fox tells how she felt about writing as a child, how she feels about it as an adult, and why she writes. It is a good follow-up to her children's books and a good lead-in to having the children write about how *they* feel about writing.

Enjoying Tall Tales/Folktales/"Pourquoi" Tales

Tall tales and folktales, especially "pourquoi" tales, appeal to children and prepare them for better understanding the concept of retelling stories. By using several variations of the same folktale or tall tale, children are able to see how stories change according to who is telling them and how exaggerations often grow with each retelling. I talk with children about how such stories are "handed down" from one person to another and from one generation to another, and how what one person remembers—or chooses to tell—is not always the same as what another person remembers or tells. I particularly like to use various tall tales about Paul Bunyan and Babe the Blue Ox, as well as those about Pecos Bill and John Henry, to help children begin to realize that authors often choose to make stories their own by adding their own touches.

Folktales allow children a glimpse into the heritage and traditions of people from cultures different from their own. These stories, primarily handed down through the oral tradition, are rich with language and form, enabling children to hear a good story with a short, fast-moving plot. They are not only enjoyable but also help to "stretch" children's imaginations.

Some stories in the folktale category are "pourquoi" tales—stories that explain why certain customs or traits of people or animals have come to be. Children especially love these and enjoy creating their own. One of my favorites in this category is "Awful Aardvark" (Mwalimu and Kennaway 1989, Mwalimu 1995), which tells why aardvarks sleep in the day and hunt for food at night. Though out of print now, this delightful tale may be found in libraries, through specialty out-of-print book search organizations, or in anthologies of literature, such as the 1995 Harcourt Brace version cited above. (See Appendix B for locating out-of-print books and Appendix J for libraries and sources of literature anthologies.)

LITERATURE EXAMPLES (TALL TALES):

Paul Bunyan
retold and illustrated by Steven Kellogg (1986a)

Pecos Bill
retold and illustrated by Steven Kellogg (1986b)

Kellogg's action-packed style and vivid pictures make these two books immediate hits with young readers. Both books are full of humor and energy. They demonstrate well the exaggeration for which tall tales are known and are especially good examples of this genre. It is helpful to pair these books with other versions of the same legendary heroes so that children can compare and contrast the various authors' and illustrators' styles. These two books are excellent for stimulating picture book retellings of these far-fetched stories.

John Henry
retold by Julius Lester (1994), illustrated by Jerry Pinkney

This colorful and exciting version of the tale about John Henry won the Caldecott Honor Medal for Pinkney's bold illustrations. The story is about a powerful African-American "steel-drivin' man" so strong that he entered a contest against a steam drill to build a railroad across the country. Compare Lester's version of the story to the next one cited here.

John Henry: An American Legend
written and illustrated by Ezra Jack Keats (1987)

This reprint edition of the 1965 original text features the adventures of John Henry in a rhythmic picture book format, using large, powerful figures with bold colors. Comparing and contrasting this version to the previous listing allows children to use Venn diagrams, a comparison matrix (see Appendix C), a split step book (see illustration, right), or a flip book with one version on the top flaps and the other beneath. (See Chapter 3 and Appendixes F and G for information about step and flip books.)

Using Multicultural Literature

Multicultural literature is coming into wider use in classrooms today. It is important that teachers look for and have available in their classrooms examples of good literature that is culturally authentic for various ethnic groups. Children should see themselves, their cultural heritage, and the cultural heritage of others represented in high-quality literature. Look for multicultural literature that portrays the culture appropriately and accurately, not in a stereotypical fashion. It is important not only to represent various cultures authentically and in an unbiased manner, but also to be aware of the gender, religious, and age appropriateness of literature and other materials used in the classroom. Good literature gives us an opportunity to teach our students to respect people who are different from themselves. We must look for ways to affirm diversity and to teach our children that everyone contributes to the culture of our classroom and of our world.

Excellent examples of literature that represent various cultures, genders, religions, and ages are less available than other types of literature, so you must search harder to find them. According to Huck, Hepler, Hickman, and Kiefer (1997, page 484), you should be aware of certain considerations when evaluating multicultural books, such as a diverse representation of members of that culture. For example, look for wide ranges of occupations, educational backgrounds, lifestyles, and living conditions. These experts also caution teachers to pay attention to the overall perspective taken by the book, including language and stereotyping. Other sources that give more detailed guidelines can be found in Augusta Baker's (1984) *The Black Experience in Children's Books*, and Rudine Sims's (1982) *Shadow and Substance: Afro-American Experience in Contemporary Children's Fiction*. Additionally, there are web sites that specifically direct their users to various sources of good literature from many cultures (see Appendix J). Also refer to the cooking section of Chapter 5 for ways to introduce cultures through foods and literature.

LITERATURE EXAMPLES FROM ONE CULTURAL GROUP (AFRICAN-AMERICAN ETHNICITY):

Honey, I Love
by Eloise Greenfield (1978), illustrated by Jan Spivey Gilchrist

This "Let's Read Aloud" version of Greenfield's poem provides a heartwarming representation of an African-American girl's family and the things she loves about them. The poem, featured in Greenfield's *Honey, I Love and Other Love Poems* (1972), was discussed earlier in the section on using poetry with children. I mention it in this section because this particular version is a good example of high-quality African-American literature. It is interesting for children to compare the format of this version of the poem with the one in her other book. As Jim Trelease reminds readers who use read-alouds such as this one, "story does not exist to teach reading skills. Story is the vehicle we use to make sense out of the world. . . ." (1989, page 57). This wonderful read-aloud is one of the best picture books for children of any ethnicity because of its theme and the feelings it evokes. Children can use it to create their own parallel picture book poem.

The Paperboy
written and illustrated by Dav Pilkey (1996)

This Caldecott Honor Book depicts a young African-American boy who delivers papers when the mornings are still dim and cool. It shows the hard work of this youngster and explains the duties of a paperboy in terms that young readers understand. The dark paintings convey the feeling of early morning before the world is astir. Children read this book and see applications to their own lives. They realize that they have a story to tell through pictures and words, just like the paperboy. This is a good model for telling a story in a step-by-step manner. It is also an outstanding example of African-American literature that portrays its character appropriately through both the text and illustrations.

The illustrations lend themselves to working with children in creating similar night/early morning scenes. The sky is painted in deep shades of purple, blue, or black, with stars and moon painted yellow. The grass and houses are shaded with black to give the appearance of darkness. A yellow light beams from the light on the bicycle. The words are written in light pastel colors on a dark background. Then, as the world "wakes up" little by little, the sky becomes bright orange and magenta, followed by the bright orange and yellow sky of full morning, as the paperboy and his dog head back home and into the boy's bed for some much-needed sleep.

ACTIVITY: Once they have a story written, children could create a similar picture book using a crayon-resist art technique. They draw their illustrations on photocopier paper (which holds up well) by coloring very hard (holding crayons near the tip to keep them from snapping) with light- or bright-colored crayons. Next, they write the words of their story in yellow, white, light pink, light blue, or silver crayon (again, pressing down very hard to leave as much wax as possible on the paper so that the paint/water wash will bubble off the wax-covered areas and allow the color of the crayon to show through). Then, to give the effect of darkness, children use wide (at least 2") paintbrushes dipped into the top of a jar of very watery black paint, going across the entire surface of the paper. (They should not dip their brushes into the bottom of the jar because paint may have settled there and become too thick to produce the desired very thin wash of color.) Painting should move left to right with one broad continuous stroke, starting at the top of the paper and gradually covering the page from top to bottom—over words, pictures . . . everything—using consistent brush strokes that overlap as little as possible so that no area of the picture receives too much paint.

Open large garbage bags and tape them over the top of the painting table to protect it. Spread newspapers in layers so that as each child paints, the top layer can be removed to allow the next child to begin with a relatively clean surface. Gather old, short-sleeve, button-up-the-front, adult-size shirts to serve as paint cover-ups to protect children's clothing. Let children put on the shirts with buttons to the back, having a friend fasten one top button to keep the shirt in place. (By wearing one myself, I eliminate the children's resistance to these

odd-looking paint smocks, while protecting my own clothes too!)

I gather the class around the paint table as I mix a paint/water wash, combining approximately one part of black tempera paint with two parts of water so that students know how to make it themselves later. Then I demonstrate how to hold the crayon at the tip to keep it from snapping, how to color hard, and how to paint across the entire paper so the paint will bubble off the crayon. (Some children want to paint around their drawings, but we talk about the fact that water does not adhere to wax and that if they color *hard* there will be enough wax on the surface of the paper to make the wash bead up so that their pictures show through clearly. If they color too lightly, the paint will cover their work.)

I put one child in charge of the paint table as the "captain" for the day. That child's job is to keep the painting going smoothly—to check each child's picture to be sure that the crayon is dark enough to resist the paint; to remind each child how to cover the surface of his/her picture with broad, smooth brush strokes; to remind children to dip their paintbrushes only into the *top* of the wash; to move finished paintings to the drying surface (in our case, to the newspaper-covered floor under the radiators); and to remove the paint-soaked newspapers, leaving fresh paper for the next participant.

I usually let two to four students paint at a time, depending upon how rushed we are that day. Each child who leaves the table picks another child who has finished his/her picture and is working as instructed. The shirt is passed to that child, with the one who receives the shirt unbuttoning the button for the one who is passing it on, and then the giver of the shirt fastening the button for the one who receives it. This works very smoothly and keeps me from being tied up at the paint table. Even young children are quite capable of running this operation by themselves, needing help only for occasional spills.

"More, More, More," Said the Baby: 3 Love Stories
written and illustrated by Vera B. Williams (1990)

This Caldecott Honor Book is an excellent story to use with young children as an illustration of the way scenes can be depicted through illustrations as much as through words. The bright art and colorful text in the large-format hardcover edition are especially appealing as they portray babies of three cultures in wonderfully appropriate ways. The watercolor pictures show chubby, wiggly, irresistible Little Guy, Little Pumpkin, and Little Bird calling for "more, more, more!" as they run giggling, only to be scooped up by loving adults who swing them around, kiss them, rock them, and tuck them into bed. The simple refrain invites children to participate in reading this bright picture book and to use refrains in their own writing, while at the same time showing that babies are valued, cuddled, and enjoyed by families—no matter what the culture.

Shades of Black: A Celebration of Our Children
by Sandra L. Pinkney (2000), photographs by Myles C. Pinkney

This 2000 publication celebrates children of color, specifically African-Americans. The bright, clear photos show children of every hue. The Pinkneys use appealing terms to describe their hair, their eyes, and their skin tones: "vanilla," "butter pecan," "chocolate," "coppery brown." My favorite page is the last:

> I am **Black**
>
> I am Unique
>
> I come from ancient Kings and Queens.
>
> When you look at me, what do you see?
>
> I am Black
>
> I am proud to be me

This charming book captivates all who study it—playing with the sounds of the words and enjoying the pictures of beautiful black children engaged in everyday activities to which we can all relate. It is a winner! Children can use their own photos and words to create similar class books to share with families and friends.

EXPLORING LITERATURE OF THE LOCAL CULTURE

One of the types of literature that I would not want to forget to use with my students is that of the culture of our locality. In my classrooms throughout various parts of the country, I have tried to include examples of regional literature. Since moving to Louisiana, I have discovered new favorites to share with my students. In addition to the books listed below, there are two exciting storytelling web sites (see Appendix J, page 193) that feature storytellers and video clips of some of them telling their favorite stories. I encourage you to explore both sites.

LITERATURE EXAMPLES—A SAMPLING OF CULTURES (LOUISIANA *LAGNIAPPE*, "A LITTLE SOMETHING EXTRA"):

A Cajun Little Red Riding Hood
written and illustrated by Berthe Amoss (2000)

This version of the familiar *Little Red Riding Hood* fairy tale is full of specific Cajun words and the rhythm and flavor of the speech of the Acadiana region of Louisiana, making it one of my personal favorites. The reader is constantly called "Cher" (the Cajun term for "Dear") by the unseen teller of the tale, drawing readers/listeners into a closer connection with the story as she takes us into her confidence, divulging to us all the "juicy details," just as a local storyteller would do. Little Red Riding Hood's grandmother is called "Mere," and the wolf is replaced by the dreaded "M'sieur Cocodrie" of Louisiana bayous and swamps—Mr. Alligator— whose colorful cardboard cutout can be moved through slits in the pages to captivate all who watch as he plots and connives.

A guide to pronunciations at the end of the book aids the reader with local dialect. I made a tape of a friend reading this delightful tale in her broad, rhythmic vernacular and practiced reading it until I could share the story with children in a way that sounds "just right." An added bonus is cooking "Mère's Secret Recipe for Pralines" (PRAW-leans), given at the end of the book!

It is beneficial to have children compare this version with the traditional tale, as well as with another cultural adaptation, the 1990 Caldecott Award winner *Lon Po Po: A Red Riding Hood Story from China*, adapted and illustrated by Young (1989). Following such comparisons, young authors find it easier to create their own cultural adaptations and later to share them, paying attention to likenesses and differences between their versions and the others.

ACTIVITY: Create class or group Venn diagrams comparing and contrasting versions of the *Little Red Riding Hood* tales the class has read and written. Post these comparisons in the hall with the caption: "Wanted: More *Little Red Riding Hood* Stories—Send Us Your Best!" (Be sure to leave room to include versions and/or comparisons from other classes.)

Cajun Gingerbread Boy
rebaked and illustrated by Berthe Amoss (1999)

Follow *A Cajun Little Red Riding Hood* with Amos's equally delightful *Cajun Gingerbread Boy*. Have children compare the author/illustrator's work in the two books. M'sieur Cocodrie again slithers through the tale, this time with the Gingerbread Boy doing the running. It is helpful to try to find a real Louisiana teacher/storyteller to read this story onto a tape, which you can then place in a listening center in the classroom. Ask the children to compare the two tales by Amoss.

The Talking Eggs: A Folktale from the American South
by Robert D. San Souci (1989), illustrated by Jerry Pinkney

This Caldecott Honor Book, also a Coretta Scott King Award Honor Book, is another interesting Louisiana folktale, this one adapted from a Creole story. Children enjoy the combination of San Souci's humorous, spirited retelling with Pinkney's full-page illustrations. Comparing this retelling with the characters in traditional fairy tales such as "Cinderella" and "Snow White and Rose Red" leads to some lively discussions. The tale, told as if it happened "down Louisiana way long ago," appeals to children and grown-ups alike. Ask your students to retell or create their own version.

Retellings Based Upon Literature

Retellings are stories that are retold in the words of a listener who has heard a story or a reader who has read a story. It is helpful for young children to have heard a particular version of a story more than once before they attempt to retell it. This procedure is based on Hazel Brown and Brian Cambourne's (1987) description of appreciating literature through retelling. The procedure is fully described in their book *Read and Retell: A Strategy for the Whole-Language/Natural Learning Classroom.* There are many benefits to children from the use of the retelling procedure as they use all of the language arts in combination for intensive listening, speaking, reading, and writing about a particular topic. The sharing and comparing component of a retelling lesson involves multiple readings and rereadings of the original text as well as the retelling text. Brown and Cambourne cite their observation of students' growth through using retellings in the areas of knowledge of text forms and conventions, consciousness concerning the processes involved in construction of text, carryover of text forms and conventions to other writing tasks, control of vocabulary, flexibility in reading, and confidence (pages 11–12).

A quick version of a simple retelling procedure is as follows: Read and reread a text to children over a period of several days, reflecting upon that text and discussing it between readings. After the second reading (or the third for more difficult stories), ask the children to write everything they can remember about the story. They can do their written retellings in their reading logs; but retellings are usually lengthy, so I generally have students write them on regular notebook paper so I can take them home in a less-bulky form to read and consider. It is good to have children try to recall specific features of the story they are retelling, such as "storybook" (figurative) language, characters, setting, and exact sequence of events. It is truly amazing how many details children can remember. Second graders are able to do written retellings with much accuracy, though they usually tire before writing everything they can remember about a story. Invariably, during the sharing of the retellings the young authors remember more details and add them to their written efforts. Kindergartners and first graders can orally retell on tape for later transcription by adults. These may be typed and shared with classmates. In addition, the children may wish to illustrate them before sharing.

Another book describing ways to support retellings in classrooms of children in grades K–3 is *The Power of Retelling: Developmental Steps for Building Comprehension*, by Vicki Benson and Carrice Cummins (2000). This is a valuable addition to professional libraries of early childhood teachers. The particular strategies that these two authors recommend help children gain expertise in retelling from literature. In brief, they suggest using props and pictures to support retellings when children are first learning to do them. They also suggest a continuum of scaffolds that gradually decrease outside support for young writers until they are able to do retellings on their own.

Because of the intense effort required to sustain such a lengthy written piece, a written retelling from literature is a strategy that is best used at widely spaced intervals for very young children. It is, however, one of the more worthwhile and rewarding types of writing with children of any age. Retellings have had an important impact on my students and me, both in building classroom community and in scaffolding literacy development. Three children's books that are excellent resources for retellings are *Awful Aardvark* (Mwalimu and Kennaway 1989, Mwalimu 1995), *The Wolf's Chicken Stew* (Kasza 1987), and *The Day Jimmy's Boa Ate the Wash* (Noble 1980). I describe these retellings in Stewart (in press).

It is important to occasionally use books that are themselves retellings so children realize that "real" authors do retellings, too. Good examples are Steven Kellogg's retellings of tall tales, such as those mentioned in the section entitled "Enjoying Tall Tales/Folktales/'Pourquoi' Tales" (see page 86), because the books' covers mention that the books are retold and illustrated by Kellogg (see Kellogg 1986a, 1986b).

LITERATURE EXAMPLES:

Where the Wild Things Are
written and illustrated by Maurice Sendak (1984)

This picture book captures children's imaginations as they hear about Max's dreamland trip to the place where the wild things are. The story makes an excellent source for children's retellings as they try to capture the flavor, vivid vocabulary, and pictures of Sendak's award-winning book.

Goldilocks and the Three Bears
retold and illustrated by Jan Brett (1987)

A retelling itself of the well-known fairy tale, this book has a few subtle variations on the more familiar versions, as well as pictures which are appealing to young children. It is enlightening to have children do a retelling of this particular version of *Goldilocks and the Three Bears* to see if they are retelling from Brett's book or from another one they have heard before. Those children who are tuned-in to this version pick up the subtle storybook language, as well as details, such as the lifting of the latch, the beds that were too high at the head or too low at the foot, and other interesting details. When children read and share their retellings aloud, they frequently notice things they have left out or misplaced. When given the chance, they are usually able to insert those changes. (See Appendix I for a student's first-draft retelling of Jan Brett's tale.)

The Legend of the Poinsettia
retold and illustrated by Tomie dePaola (1994)

As children hear the Mexican legend of how the poinsettia came to be, they become aware of how legends are attached to holiday customs and symbols. This story is a good source for a retelling, a picture book, or a play. Point out that the book itself is a retelling by a famous author who took someone else's story and retold it through his own eyes. This also is an excellent example of culturally appropriate multicultural literature.

Littlejim's Gift: An Appalachian Christmas Story
by Gloria Houston (1994), illustrated by Thomas B. Allen

This touching story about the true meaning of Christmas sparks a discussion with children about Christmas as a time of giving. It is a good vehicle for getting children to write about ways we can give to others during this holiday. The story is rich with details and full of warm Christmas feelings, inspiring children to explore their own feelings and memories of Christmas traditions. Written or taped retellings are very effective when used with this story. Allow struggling writers to sit in an isolated area of the classroom with their back to the class and tell the story into the microphone of a tape recorder. It is often rewarding for the children to hear the tape played aloud. Many times I type particularly good taped retellings, put them on a transparency (with the child's permission), and play the tape for the class while viewing the transparency. Then we discuss the strengths of that piece. Usually this helps reluctant writers move toward the next step in the process—that of writing the retelling for themselves. Invite a storyteller in to share their retellings of favorite stories, especially during the Christmas season, as a follow-up to this book. This is another example of good multicultural literature.

DEVELOPING PARALLEL STORIES

Parallel stories are based upon someone else's original writing. They are particularly good for introducing children to writing books because the children can take an author's original idea and then change or expand it in some way to make a new version of an especially appealing story line.

CIRCULAR TALES:

These are stories that have a beginning, go through a series of events, and return to the starting point. Children enjoy hearing and writing parallel versions of circular stories, or stories-in-the-round. This may be done individually, with partners or small groups, or as an entire class.

ACTIVITY: A good way to have children write a circular tale is to cut out a large circle from poster board or chart paper. (This is a good project for a team of two children to undertake together.) After they have drawn their circle and cut it out (or had it cut out by the teacher if they are too young to manage this for themselves), the children create illustrations for each event that happened in the story. They glue these illustrations around the edges of the circle as a way of retelling the story. This activity lends itself to an oral retelling in which the children point to their illustrations and tell what happened at each point in the story. The fact that the events are depicted around the circumference of the circle helps the children visualize the story as a "circular" tale that begins at one point, goes through a series of events,

and returns to the same starting point. I like to have the children stand together and share their oral retelling with the class. Sometimes we audiotape the retellings (and/or create written versions as well). We place the large circle with the illustrations on the wall and put a small table beneath them with a tape player and headsets so the children can listen to the tapes while they look at the circle. For my second graders, a third step was to create written versions that we also kept on the table.

Another way is to have children create their own picture books based on a particular circular story. To bring out the revolving nature of these stories, punch a hole in the upper left corner of students' books and insert a binding ring. As children flip pages to share their stories, they see that they go through the series of events, coming back to the start.

LITERATURE EXAMPLES:

If You Give a Mouse a Cookie
by Laura Joffe Numeroff (1985), illustrated by Felicia Bond

If You Give a Moose a Muffin
by Laura Joffe Numeroff (1991), illustrated by Felicia Bond

These two circular tales are concerned with a central animal character who wants a food item, which, when obtained, sends him to find something else, and on and on until he returns to the first item. Children have fun reading these books and easily write circular stories of their own after hearing them. Numeroff's stories work well early in the year as a model for whole-class stories. Ask each student to illustrate a page of the whole-class-created parallel version of the story.

Repeated Phrase Books:

Alexander's Terrible, Horrible, No Good, Very Bad Day
by Judith Viorst (1972), illustrated by Ray Cruz

One morning, after having a minor fender-bender on the way to school, I came into class saying that I had a book that I needed to share with my students so that they would understand the beginning of my day. I took the time to read this book to the children, encouraging them to chime in on the refrain, "It was a terrible, horrible, no good, very bad day." Then I modeled writing the beginning of a book about my own "terrible, horrible, no good, very bad day." (I had purposely saved this activity for a day that *did* have a bad beginning.) Next, I had the children write books about their own "terrible, horrible, no good, very bad day." I told them they might end every page with the words, "It was a terrible, horrible, no good, very bad day" or the opposite: "It was a super fantastic, absolutely wonderful, totally terrific, very good day." This was a well-received activity and one which engendered *much* discussion as we shared our stories!

Riddle Books:

What Am I?
by Margaret Hillert (1981), illustrated by Sharon Elzaurdia

This very simple riddle book helps students understand what a riddle is and how to write one. Hillert uses simple riddles and easy vocabulary accompanied by Elzaurdia's bright and appealing illustrations.

ACTIVITY: After sharing this book as a read-aloud, I ask each child to write a two-page riddle. The first page consists of three short clues and a question—"What am I?"—together with a picture that gives a hint but does not include the described item. The second page tells the answer and includes a descriptive follow-up, such as a "hat," "a tall black hat," as well as a picture of the item. Compile the children's riddles to make a class book (see Figure 8).

Page One (Front)	Page Two (Back)
I grow on a tree.	An apple . . .
I taste sweet and juicy.	A shiny, red apple.
I am crunchy and red.	
What am I?	
	Construction hint:
	Be sure to put the answer page on the back of the question page—not on facing pages.

Figure 8. Example of a riddle book

USING LITERATURE WITH YOUNG CHILDREN

In summary, using literature with young children has many benefits. It enhances children's literacy experiences and serves as a basis for joint memories and enjoyable times, thus contributing to the building of classroom community. It is necessary that teachers wishing to use this strategy become knowledgeable about a variety of good children's literature sources. There are several ways to do this. Teachers can easily access information about children's literature by using the Children's Literature Web Guide, which has commentary on children's books, links to other excellent sources in the area of children's literature, and a "Lots of Lists" web address. Additionally, teachers can obtain information on the "Teachers' Choices: Best New Children's Books" in the November issue each year of *The Reading Teacher*, a journal of the International Reading Association. Also, many authors have excellent web sites of their own—Judy Blume and Patricia Polacco, among others (see Appendix J).

Good anthologies of children's literature also are available. My favorite is *Children's Literature in the Elementary School*, 6th ed. (Huck, Hepler, Hickman, and Kiefer 1997). This is an outstanding resource for school libraries and an excellent guide for teachers, parents, and librarians who purchase books for children (see Appendix J).

Another very complete resource is *Adventuring with Books: A Booklist for Pre-K–Grade 6* (Sutton and the Committee to Revise the Elementary School Booklist 1997), published by the National Council of Teachers of English. This lists each book by topic and with a short synopsis. (See Appendix J for these and other book sources, lists, and helpful Internet sites for accessing information about children's literature.)

WRITING FROM EXPERIENCE

Writing across the curriculum is an important way for students to embody their experiences, attitudes, culture, and language. While it is especially important for young children to be given many opportunities to write, it is not always easy to get them started. Writing opportunities that are based upon authentic experiences become more meaningful to students, therefore making it easier for them to write.

Just as I use the metaphor of opening and closing a drawstring bag to help children write from literature, I encourage them to use the same metaphor to strengthen their writing from experience. They "open" their writing by situating the readers in the setting, they "fill" their writing with details of the experience, and they "close" their writing by pulling their ideas together in a way that makes sense for that particular piece. This chapter is designed to give practical, field-tested ideas for writing with children about their experiences.

As students attempt to convey their thoughts and impressions to others, anticipating a ready, accepting audience, they are usually willing to invest time and energy in that effort. Thus, many students become self-motivated learners as they write about what they know in the attempt to share this with those to whom they are bonded.

GETTING STARTED BY WRITING FROM CURRENT, SHARED EXPERIENCES

One of the most productive ways to get young children to write is to have them write about current experiences, especially those shared with classmates. In order to have them do this in a school setting, it is often necessary to provide a common experience for the children. This may be done in many ways, from taking an elaborate class field trip to conducting a simple science observation or experiment within the classroom to responding to shared literature. I find that taking my classes on "Elsewhere Expeditions" provides us with many rich experiences for writing. Elsewhere Expeditions are treated here as the umbrella under which aspects of student experience, attitude, culture, and language are supported. (It is advisable to discuss this activity with the principal in advance of doing it, to leave word with a neighboring teacher, and to put a note on the door giving the location of your class at all times.)

ELSEWHERE EXPEDITIONS

Elsewhere Expeditions are simple experiences with an elaborate name. Elsewhere Expeditions are *purposeful journeys* (expeditions) that occur *in another place* (elsewhere), outside the classroom. Usually, the first—and easiest—Elsewhere Expeditions I take with students are simple daily walks around the grounds of the school. We *always* set a purpose for our expeditions, such as hunting for insects, leaves, or roots, etc. This gives our expedition importance, elevating it from what could be an exercise in teacher control to purposeful inquiry by young investigators.

Most of the time our early expeditions occur in conjunction with our daily walk to the physical education class. We simply leave our classroom about 5, 10, or 15 minutes before we are due on the P.E. grounds, taking an extended route to get there, yet never leaving the premises of the school. We look for everything we can, taking time for the students to verbally point out their observations along the way. By the time we have reached the P.E. grounds, most children have pointed out at least one observation that they feel is important for some reason.

When the students are having their snack time after returning from P.E., I sit at the computer (whose screen I have turned so the class can see it) and type out a few short paragraphs as the children dictate their observations to me. While finishing their snacks, they begin drawing illustrations to accompany the dictated paragraphs. We title these "Notes from Our Elsewhere Expedition" and include the date. We then hang these daily entries outside our door for others to view (see Figure 9, page 105). Usually, before too many days have passed, children or teachers from other classes stop by our room to comment on our notes, sometimes telling us that they saw something we did not see or asking us to look for something specific as we journey out the next time.

Figure 9. Class notes following daily Elsewhere Expeditions

TEACHING NOTE-TAKING SKILLS

Once we have established the habit of observing, sharing, and reporting what we have seen, we go to the next step. We want to take notes of our expeditions, so we must learn how to do that. One of the best aids to note taking that I have ever used is the video *Mr. Know-It-Owl's Video School: All About Animals* (1986). This is a simple video, designed to introduce very young children to several animal groups—specifically, mammals, fish, amphibians, reptiles, and birds. The segments are each about 10 minutes long, with Mr. Know-It-Owl (a puppet character) explaining the groups to Scooter McGruder (another puppet character). (See Appendix B for purchasing information.)

Mr. Know-It-Owl uses video clips of wonderful live-animal shots with catchy tunes describing characteristics of the group and words that are flashed on the screen for several seconds. Children are able to grasp the concept of note taking while they copy the words on the screen as the tune tells about the animals. (Usually, I write the category, such as mammals, on the board as it is introduced in the video and write each word for those who are unable to write quickly enough to copy it before it leaves the screen.)

While watching the video, the students open their science logs (spiral notebooks work best), and I ask them to copy the words from the video onto the left-hand page and to make drawings of the animals on the right-hand page (see Figure 10). I often encourage them to write as many animal names or characteristics as they can in each category. Because this is usually the first experience my second graders have had with note taking, I show the same 10-minute segment of the video two or three times in a row so that they can check their notes. The number of viewings depends upon the ability and experience of my students. I show them no more than one animal group per day in order to minimize confusion about the groups, and I usually allow more than one day between viewings. (We also review our notes about the previous group before going on to the next.) I do not worry about misspellings at this first-draft stage but later have the children correct them, as this may become a source for their future writings.

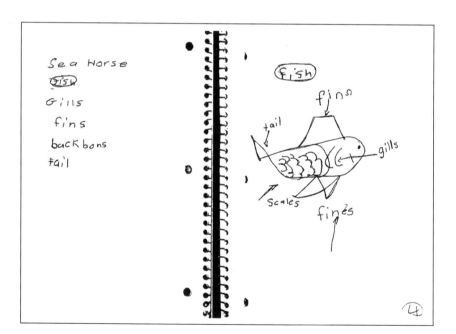

Figure 10. Early note taking in science log

The next step for my second graders is to transfer this note-taking skill to our Elsewhere Expedition experiences. By this time we are beginning to refer to our trips in our notes as E.E.'s—short for Elsewhere Expeditions. We sometimes have to miss a few days here and there because of schedule interruptions, etc., but the habit of going out of the classroom is strongly ingrained. We know that we are going somewhere for some specific purpose, and we know that we are going to write about it in some way. I generally tell them that they are such good writers that I am sure they do not need me to write up the trips any longer. I convince the students that they are already good note takers because of the notes they have taken from Mr. Know-It-Owl's videos.

Armed with clipboards, science logs, and pencils, we set out for our first "serious" E.E. (see Figure 11). Usually by this time, we have been studying our community and discussing various types of community helpers, different styles of housing, several kinds of transportation, etc. So when we set out to take notes the first time, I usually have the students write about *everything* they see on that day—scientific observations of animals and animal habitats, observations of types of housing, types of transportation, and types of community helpers. If we see community helpers, we stop to interview them about what they are doing if they are willing to talk with us.

Figure 11. Children headed out on an Elsewhere Expedition

One of the most interesting of our E.E. interviews came on the day that we observed a bus maintenance worker, "Mr. Randy," measuring the tread on our bus tires. (The children, so observant in their note taking, knew his name because of the label "Randy" on his shirt pocket, which I had not even noticed!) I asked him if he would let the children interview him about his job—particularly about what he was doing that day. Mr. Randy agreed, and the students bombarded him with questions, taking notes all the while (see Figure 12).

Figure 12. Close-up of children's drawings of "Mr. Randy" under the school bus from Elsewhere Expedition hall notes

We often take photographs (instant photography works well because of immediate results) as the children are collecting, observing, writing, reading, planning, collaborating, etc. We return to the classroom to sort our finds; to discuss our expedition; and to plan follow-up research, activities, and writings. At this point I often have the students get into groups and jot down more notes, make plans with peers, and generally begin a study of whatever the expedition uncovered. Different groups and individuals go in different directions with their projects according to their interests, but all have a connection to the focus of the expedition.

Elsewhere Expeditions are versatile and may be adapted to almost any subject area. In most instances, Elsewhere Expeditions are integrated curriculum at its best, turning up again and again in the classroom following the reading of a story when students make comments such as, "Oh, that's like what we saw on our Elsewhere Expedition last week! Do you remember . . . ?" Vocabulary is enriched and attention to detail is strengthened. Children are given the opportunity to observe nature firsthand and to reflect upon that experience as they write about it.

The following sections address ways of encouraging students to become effective, proficient writers across various academic areas. These examples of Elsewhere Expeditions have been particularly successful and show the effectiveness of creating a common experience for students in a given class.

ELSEWHERE EXPEDITIONS FOR SCIENCE

Science Example One: Insect Hunt

First the children determine (or are given) the focus for the expedition. A most successful science expedition in our classroom was one in which we went out onto the school grounds to collect insects. On this particular day, the expedition was taken earlier in the afternoon, not on our way to P.E., so that we would have sufficient time to collect insects and begin studying them.

Each student was given a Ziplock bag in which to collect insects. We went outside to various locations under a large magnolia tree, by the fence, in flower beds, and in other places on our school grounds that appeared to be rich hiding places for insects. We took instant pictures of the collection efforts (see Figure 13).

Figure 13. Collecting insects during a science Elsewhere Expedition

As students found insects, they put them into their bags for safekeeping. Once we had exhausted several choice locations and all students seemed to have their "bugs," we returned to the classroom. Each child dropped an alcohol-soaked cotton ball into the bag for insect preservation and sealed the bag shut.

The children were then divided into three groups. One group sat together, observing their insects, taking notes on appearance, and making detailed drawings in their notes. Another group sat at a large table with the Polaroid snapshots, writing about the sequence of the collecting trip, trying to remember as many details as they could. The third group sat together reading nonfiction books about the insects they had collected and taking notes from those books (see Figures 14–16).

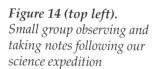

Figure 14 (top left).
Small group observing and taking notes following our science expedition

Figure 15 (top right).
Small group checking photos for details and sequence during write-up of science expedition

Figure 16 (bottom).
Small group reading nonfiction texts and taking notes as follow-up to science expedition

When our eighth-grade "helper" came in the next afternoon and for several afternoons after that, he helped the students glue their specimens onto cards and look at them through the microscope. Again, students took notes on their experience. The groups rotated, with each one getting to observe, write, and read in each of the three settings.

For many weeks we used that Elsewhere Expedition as the basis of a study of insects. As our culminating experience, we wrote a class story retelling what we did. We followed our usual procedure for writing a group story, with the children drawing illustrations on quarter sheets of photocopier paper. For that story, each student drew two small pictures—one of the outside experience and one of the inside experience. These drawings, together with the snapshots and the cards on which the insects were mounted, were glued around the class story, which we later displayed in the hall for other classes to see (see Figure 17).

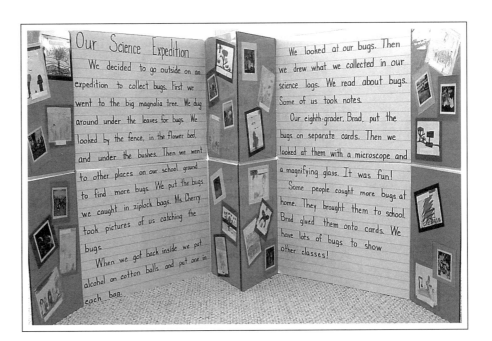

Figure 17. Whole-group story written following science expedition

Science Example Two: Animal Show

Another successful Elsewhere Expedition in science involved the school-sponsored animal show. Every year a wild animal exhibitor and his wife visit our school to share information about wild animals and to present their specimens to our student body. The entire school meets in the gym for this presentation.

Before the animal show, I asked the children to create a web with their predictions of what they expected to see this year. Because most of them had attended similar presentations during their kindergarten and first-grade years, they were confident about predicting. I asked those students who had not previously seen the show to predict what they thought they *might* see at an animal show. We made our webs on 11" x 14" sheets of construction paper, and then shared them with the group.

After we returned from the animal show, we looked again at our predictions and determined which were correct and which were incorrect. Students then wrote picture books about five favorite animals, including at least one sentence about each to tell a fact that they had learned about that animal. Then we shared the picture books.

ELSEWHERE EXPEDITIONS FOR SOCIAL STUDIES

Social Studies Example One: Lunchroom Tour

For the last several years, I have arranged with the lunchroom manager of our school cafeteria to take my students "in the back," as the children call it. When we were studying career and community helpers, I invited her to come into the classroom to speak with the students about her job. Then, within the next day or two, we followed her visit with a lunchroom tour.

This Elsewhere Expedition, easy to arrange and cost-free, had positive results for writing! The students reaped several benefits from the trip. They were given a tour through the back during which they saw community helpers in action as the lunchroom workers began preparation for the day's lunch. They gained an idea of the effort and equipment needed in preparing food for such a large school (approximately 1,400 students in the elementary and high school combined ate there daily). A side benefit was that following the trip, I rarely—if ever—heard complaints about the food. Students were amazed at the size of everything. They had a chance to explore math as we converted lunchroom recipes to family-size portions. They had a chance to take notes (see Figure 18), write from notes, and attend to sequence and details in their writing. I noticed one student numbering his writing about the lunchroom tour, so I asked him why he was doing this. He looked at me as if I should know, saying, "I *have* to number it. I'm making an outline of what we did. You know . . . it's like a *list*. I *have* to have numbers!"

Figure 18. Students taking notes during our lunchroom Elsewhere Expedition

I also used this trip as the introduction to the friendly-letter format (one of the mandated second-grade skills for our state). The students had an authentic purpose for writing those letters and really worked to express their thoughts. (Refer back to Figure 1, page 39, for examples of rough drafts of some of the letters.) The lunchroom manager and workers enjoyed our enthusiasm for all aspects of the behind-the-scenes world of the cafeteria. This positive experience helped bond the children and the lunchroom workers, resulting in hugs and smiles on subsequent journeys as we went into the lunchroom for our daily meals.

Social Studies Example Two: Home Culture/Individual Interview

Another successful Elsewhere Expedition can be accomplished by letting the children check out the camera to take home on an individual E.E. in order to bring their family culture and customs to our classroom. By interviewing, taking notes, taking photos, and then writing up their experiences, the children not only share two aspects of social studies—their families and their culture—but also use technology and writing (as well as reading, while sharing their completed projects) in an authentic way. This same technique can be used to bring careers into the classroom through student interviews.

In order to prepare my students for interviewing family and/or community members, we practice interviewing each other in class. I briefly interview small groups of children several times before I ask them to conduct an interview. This helps them become comfortable with the interviewing process, know how to operate the tape player, see how to work from a list of prepared questions, and practice taking notes as each person responds. Then I have pairs of children take turns sitting in a corner and tape recording their interview sessions so they can later hear their questions and the responses of the interviewee.

I listen to the tapes and select two interviews that are particularly well done. I ask the partner team for permission to share their tape with the class. Then, as a group, we listen to the interviews and talk about why they were good ones. I ask the children to follow our discussion by working with a partner to generate questions they want to ask.

Each child then prepares a list of questions—which can be the same as or similar to the questions generated by the pair. Individuals turn in their questions to me, and I give them feedback. Then they prepare their final draft to take with them as they interview family or community members. The children are engaged during this lengthy process because they really need to be able to remember what they want to ask. Depending upon the class, I vary the length of time this process takes—usually one or two days, sometimes longer.

ELSEWHERE EXPEDITIONS FOR MATH

Math Example One: Shape Search

Guiding the students through the school and/or school grounds to look for geometric shapes in the environment is interesting. I usually assign the students to groups, with a photographer, an artist (or two), and several note takers. Then, for the next several days, the group works up a project to share their findings with the class. The students are frequently secretive, not wanting other groups to find the same things. It is most successful when I stay in the classroom with the majority of my students and send out one group at a time with an instructional assistant, secretary, office worker, or parent. When that is not possible, I take the entire group outside, letting the majority of the class face me as I read to them. A small group, ever in my sight, works at a distance from the main group. Across a period of several days, all groups have an opportunity to prepare their projects. Group projects are shared when all have been completed.

Math Example Two: Charts and Graphs

Another way we incorporate math into the Elsewhere Expeditions is by grouping children as partners for an exploratory trip in which they count specific categories of items (buildings, trees, buses, cars, bushes, birds, sections of fencing, etc.). They return to the classroom armed with notes and, with their partners, make pictographs, charts, or bar graphs of their findings.

We also make charts and graphs based on temperature readings. Small peer groups, armed with a thermometer and clipboards, check and record the temperature in our classroom and in the shade on the way to P.E., and then leave their thermometers and clipboards atop the metal bleachers near the P.E. ground, checking and recording the temperature there at the end of P.E. class. They do this over a period of days, and then each group makes a temperature bar graph to show their findings. We also make a graph to compare the readings across the groups.

ELSEWHERE EXPEDITIONS FOR LANGUAGE ARTS

Language Arts Example One: Retelling Factual Events

Retellings are among the most productive of the Elsewhere Expeditions. As in retellings from literature (discussed in Chapter 4), retellings from a real experience bring about an immersion in language with many benefits to the writer (or teller, in the case of younger students or less able writers). Brown and Cambourne (1987) cite specific benefits and offer suggestions for those teachers wishing to conduct this procedure in their classrooms.

An adaptation of Brown and Cambourne's work is to have the children retell their actual experiences in addition to retelling the literature they have read. The procedure is much the same, but with very young children, it is even easier to encourage a retelling from an experience. For our first retelling experience we do whole-class retellings of a group experience. (Refer to Elsewhere Expeditions for Science, Example One: Insect Hunt, pages 109–111, to read about a group retelling. Refer to Figure 17, page 111, for an actual write-up.)

I particularly like the lunchroom tour mentioned earlier in this chapter as an event to be retold individually because the students are always so excited about it. Behind-the-scenes tours of the school office, library, band hall, or high school science lab also appeal to children. Tours provide excellent opportunities to stress attention to details, sequence, main idea, and summary, as well as collaboration through sharing and comparing retellings. Reflection is encouraged; vocabulary is expanded and shared; mechanics such as spelling, capitalization, and punctuation are used, proofread, and corrected. One of the most important benefits seems to be the high degree of active involvement on the part of students with various aspects of language during the written or oral retelling and the sharing of that retelling with peers.

Language Arts Example Two: Nonfiction Picture Books

Another versatile way to use writing with Elsewhere Expeditions is through use of student-created picture books. (See Chapter 4 for more about creating picture books.) This is particularly successful with beginning or poor writers. Picture books typically show a picture per page with one or two lines of text above or below the illustration. After a mini-lesson in which attention is called to the aspects of a nonfiction picture book and to the fact that many times more information may be in the illustrations than in the actual text, children quickly grasp the concept of creating informative nonfiction picture books and are usually eager to create their own.

It is helpful when writing from actual experience to have the students read and review factual text to see how "real" authors create such books. Two particularly good examples of this type of text are *Ant Cities*, by Arthur Dorros (1987), and *Spiders*, by Esther Cullen (1986). Students who learn in a mini-lesson to read labels, captions, and charts frequently use those same devices in their own books. They learn quickly that illustrations, photos, charts, labels, and captions convey a wealth of information in an easily digestible format. They learn to attend to those aspects of printed material and to include them in their writings.

Following the study of *Ant Cities*, which was in our literature basal and which I brought in trade book format as well, our class went on an E.E. for the specific purpose of studying ants. For several days we observed every anthill we could find. We read many books about ants. We even made our own ant farms by catching ants in jars and covering the

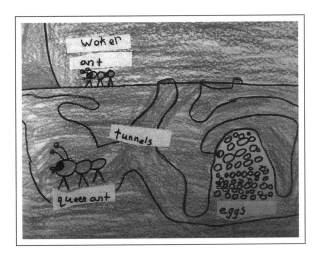

Figure 19. First-draft page of text illustration and labels from nonfiction text about ants

jars with black construction paper to provide an environment similar to what ants are used to. From that study we wrote and illustrated books with factual information (see Figure 19, page 117, and Figure 19a, below).

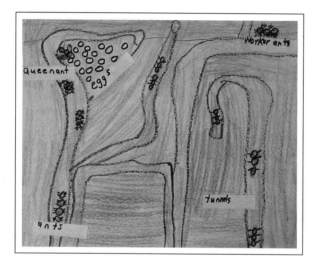

Figure 19a. *First-draft page of text illustration and labels from nonfiction text about ants*

ELSEWHERE EXPEDITIONS FOR ART

Art Example One: Nature Rubbings

An old but fascinating idea for young children is to take them outside to collect items from which to make rubbings. One day in the fall, I bring along paper lunch bags when I pick up the children after P.E. class, and take them on an extended route back to the classroom. On that walk back, each child collects whatever appeals to him or her to become the basis of an art-rubbing project, which we have discussed prior to the P.E. period. Children collect leaves, wildflowers, rocks with interesting surfaces, feathers, or any other textured objects. When we get into the classroom, they pull out their "treasures" and create a design on paper by placing one of the items under a sheet of paper and rubbing across that section of the paper with a peeled crayon, held sideways, so the long surface of the crayon rubs across the paper-covered object. Children sometimes use the same item over and over, with different placements under the paper and different colored crayons to do the rubbings. Other times they use different items to make different texture designs and vary the color or not as they desire. They share their finished products and tell how they created them.

Art Example Two: Kite Flight

A simple Elsewhere Expedition, but one of our most fun trips, occurred following an art lesson in which the children made kites. For that day's E.E., we spent time outside, running and flying our kites! The children were asked to write about the experience, and several decided to tell how it felt to fly a kite. It was a pleasant time of sharing expressive written and oral language (see Figure 20).

Figure 20. Exuberant kite-flying Elsewhere Expedition connecting art and expressive language

WRITING FROM IN-CLASS EXPERIENCES

"LEARN FROM THE EXPERT"—AFFIRMING AND BUILDING UPON PRIOR KNOWLEDGE

Not everything we experience together and write about occurs during our Elsewhere Expeditions. We make time and give attention to in-class experiences, too. For many years we did not have a formal name for these types of experiences, but the children were treated as "experts" and began to think of them as times they "learned from the expert." I am presently calling these in-class sharings with experts—whether child or adult—"Learn from the Expert" sessions.

Because each child is "the" expert for the day—and because the children have difficulty waiting for their turn to be the "expert"—I do not wait to tie in each presentation with particular units of study in science or social studies, as I would prefer to do. These sessions seem to work best for my young students when they are done in a series, such as day by day for a four- to six-week block of time.

The children tell me prior to their day as resident expert what their area of expertise will be. Then I send a note to parents/guardians, asking them to write a note to that child, stating what they like about the child. I also write a note myself and ask the children and other adults who may work with that child to do the same. Then I take time to gather supporting materials and books so I can make them available for use in the classroom when the day comes for the child's presentation. On the child's day as expert, he or she brings in items to share and makes a presentation to the class about his/her topic. Following the presentation, we present the letters to the "expert" and each of us writes another letter telling what we liked or what we learned from the presentation. Photos from the presentation and all of the letters go into a big book that is presented to the child, a copy of which stays in the class library. This activity does much to create an appreciation of every child as an expert and seems to help our classroom focus on the positives we each bring to our classroom community (see Figure 21, page 121).

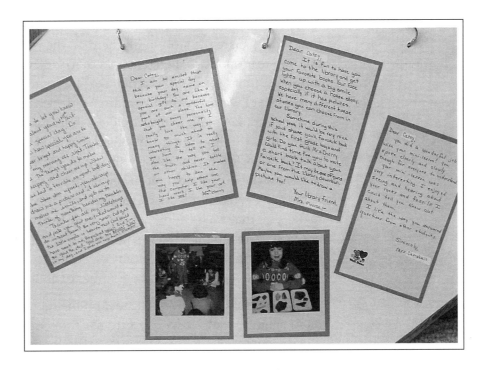

Figure 21. *Pages of class big book made following Catey's "expert" presentation on fossils*

CLASSROOM COOKING—CONNECTING EXPERIENCE, LITERATURE, AND WRITING

Classroom cooking, one of my favorite in-class experiences to set up for children, brings together many aspects of learning—engaging all of our senses as we see, smell, taste, listen, and touch throughout this activity. We can connect physical experience, oral language, math, science, social studies, literature, and writing through cooking. In this section, I share particular books that have been helpful in our classroom cooking sessions, including the reasons I particularly like each.

Stone Soup: An Old Tale
written and illustrated by Marcia Brown (1947/1975)

Stone Soup is my favorite "classroom cooking starter" because it eases children into cooking as they enjoy recreating a story from literature that has become a classic. I particularly like Marcia Brown's version of *Stone*

Soup, and have the children read along as I read it aloud two times. The first time, I share the story with them on the rug, treating this as one of my favorite read-alouds. Then, I ask them to look on the playground at P.E. for good stones for us to use to make stone soup in class. They are usually aghast that I would really use a dirty old rock from our playground to put in our soup! I explain that we will wash it at school, that I will scrub it at home, then put it in my dishwasher, then boil it until I am sure that it is totally clean. Their next job is to bring in something to put into the soup, such as a carrot, potato, onion, beans, peas, corn, salt, pepper, or garlic. Some can even bring a bit of rice or a few noodles or pieces of macaroni. I make sure that each child has something very small to contribute so it will not be a hardship on anyone's family. I bring a chunk of meat and use either my large electric skillet, my electric Crock-Pot, or a large pot and a hot plate (depending upon the number of children to be served).

As the children arrive at school on the day we cook, I read the story to them again so that we will be sure we know exactly what to do. They dictate to me a recipe for our soup, using the ingredients we have brought that day. I write the recipe on a large chart on the board so that we will be able to post it in our room for those who want to copy the recipe to make at home with their families. (We talk about why they *must* have an adult with them to cut up the vegetables and meat and to use the stove.)

Then we are ready to cook. I have placed a low table in the center of a large space so the children can gather around it. Some children are seated on low chairs around the table; others are standing behind them so that all can easily see everything. We talk about how we will take turns with our cooking so that each child has a part in making the soup. I give each child a task, from placing the stone in the pot to measuring cups of water to pouring in the water to adding the meat and vegetables to the soup. Then three different children measure and put in the seasonings and another places the lid on the pot so that it can simmer for at least an hour.

While our stone soup is simmering, we write about our experience. The children write about what they did first, next, and so on, so that they get the idea that cooking is a sequential process. I also ask them to tell how our stone soup is like that in Brown's book. What is the same? What is different?

One time when my class made stone soup, our neighbor, Mrs. Mettinger, stopped by our room on the way to taking her class to the water fountain, saying that the smell was surely making them hungry! Several of her children peeped inside to see what was going on. (Several who were in my class the year before explained what we were doing.) Then they continued down the hall. That episode started a discussion in my classroom. My students thought that it was mean to eat all the soup when Mrs. M.'s class could smell the mouthwatering aroma and that we should share it. I had some small disposable cups in my cabinet, so we decided that if we used those smaller cups we could make our soup "stretch" enough to invite Mrs. M.'s class to share it with us. We quickly made her class an invitation, which one of our students with very good handwriting printed again as a neat, final draft. A pair of students delivered it, and 30 minutes later 26 third graders entered our classroom, all smiles. We served their class first. They filed by the soup pot, where I stood, ladle in hand, to give them a taste of our stone soup. Then my students filed by, also getting a taste.

Our class wrote about the experience in many ways—stories about how we used our senses in making and eating stone soup, stories about sharing with Mrs. M.'s class, stories about how they planned to cook stone soup at home. Mrs. M.'s class used the experience to write thank-you letters to our class. All in all, this was a wonderfully productive experience for both classes. We were able to integrate cooking, literature, and writing with building class and school community. We all left that day feeling good about our time together.

The Popcorn Book
written and illustrated by Tomie dePaola (1978)

Another favorite that makes it easy to combine cooking with literature and writing is Tomie dePaola's *The Popcorn Book*. This is also a good book to use when first introducing cooking to the classroom. Through his main characters, twin brothers named Tony (who likes to cook) and Tiny (who likes to read), dePaola presents lots of information in a concise format about something they both like to do—eat popcorn! He explains what popcorn is, how to store and cook it, how Native Americans made it, and how much of it Americans eat today. Then he includes popcorn stories, legends, and recipes. DePaola uses speech "balloons" to show what the characters are saying, a technique that is beneficial to children who are just learning to use dialogue in their writing. I follow up the reading of this picture book with popping popcorn in class, letting the children eat it, and then asking them to write about it in different ways that they choose. For example, they might write a recipe for making popcorn balls, with step-by-step directions, or make a picture book, describing the senses used in making popcorn. I like to use this book in conjunction with activities around Thanksgiving, and since corn is a food used in more than one culture, it's easy to incorporate into multicultural studies as well.

Pancakes for Breakfast
by Tomie dePaola (1990)

This book also lends itself to classroom cooking. Before preparing pancakes in class (on an electric griddle or frying pan), I share this wordless picture book with my students, and then ask them to write their own version of the text. When it is introduced to the classroom after *The Popcorn Book*, children are eager to use speech balloons in their versions of the story. I usually have them retell the story as a picture book. They work in small groups, with each child responsible for a certain number of pages so that the task is more fun and not so much effort. Then we work through the writing process and end up with a completely edited and polished final draft, which I copy for each group member to keep.

Copying hint: I have the children wait to color their final drafts so that the black-and-white pictures will copy clearly. Then each child colors his or her own copy of the group's picture book.

Authorship credit: The children use the title *Pancakes for Breakfast* and give authorship credit by including the following: "Originally written by Tomie dePaola, retold by" (names of all the students in the group, listed in alphabetical order by last name), followed by the school name, city, and state on the front of the title page, with the date on the back side of the title page—the copyright page—as it would be done in a published book.

Mouse Cookies: 10 Easy-to-Make Cookie Recipes with a Story in Pictures
by Laura Numeroff & Felicia Bond (1995)

Laura Numeroff's words and Felicia Bond's pictures make this tiny cookbook a must for fans of *If You Give a Mouse a Cookie* (and *If You Give a Moose a Muffin*), written by the same author/illustrator team. I use this cookbook during the early stages of our classroom cooking for several reasons:

1) It is a logical follow-up to good literature that we have read and enjoyed together.

2) The wordless story in pictures that accompanies the recipes gives children a chance to once again provide speech balloons in which they tell the story in what *they* think the words should be.

3) There are two excellent rules for cooking just inside the front cover:

- Always wash your hands before you start cooking.

- Always have a grown-up with you when you are using the oven.

ORGANIZATIONAL HINT:

All recipes in *Mouse Cookies* require baking. I have used one or two small toaster ovens to actually bake in the classroom, but this is so time-consuming that I have found it more successful to make arrangements ahead of time with the lunchroom manager to bake the cookies in the school cafeteria's ovens. We schedule together so that our cooking does not interfere with preparations for the day's lunch.

Preparation hint: Before class, I prepare the cookie sheets by lining them with aluminum foil, which I then section off into six or eight squares (depending on the size of the cookies) by making faint lines in the surface of the foil. I then write the name of a child by each square. The children simply find their name and place their cookie dough inside their square for baking in the cafeteria

(continued)

kitchen. This works nicely. A final word of caution is that the squares should be *much* larger than the unbaked cookie dough so that when it spreads as it cooks, it will not cover the lines marking off the square or the child's name.

Lifting the cookie onto the baking sheet: If children work directly on individual pieces of aluminum foil to form their cookies, then simply snip the foil about 1½" from the edges of the cookie dough, pick up the foil piece with the dough on it, and place it on the foil-covered cookie sheet in the square with the right name on it. Sometimes when children make a cookie on another surface, such as wax paper, and then try to lift it onto the pan, the dough gets mashed,

breaks apart, or otherwise becomes deformed, causing the children frustration when they have to start over and make a new cookie. Working directly on aluminum foil eliminates this problem.

Suggestion: If you are unable to use the lunchroom and must cook with a toaster oven, it is wise to make a recipe at home first, using the same oven you plan to use in class. This way you will learn how long it takes, what temperature works best for that oven, how many cookies you can place on the tray at one time, and how much time to allow for the multiple bakings needed to serve your entire class. If this process is entirely too unwieldy, look for recipes that can be prepared with no baking.

The Peanut Butter Cookbook for Kids
by Judy Ralph and Ray Gompf (1995), illustrated by Craig Terlson

I like to use simple cookbooks with children early in the year so I can have "cooking stations" that children can manage independently at various points in our curriculum. This cookbook, which shares various ways to use peanut butter, works very well in these stations. Some of the recipes are new; others are favorites from a grandmother's collection. The recipes tell what the children will need; they call for common ingredients; and they are accompanied by detailed sketches of each phase of the step-by-step directions. Chock-full of facts and tips, the cookbook has callout sections titled "Did you know?" It can easily be connected with a science unit on plants, with children actually following directions from the cookbook on how to grow their own peanuts and make their own peanut butter!

ORGANIZATIONAL HINT:

It is helpful when cooking in the classroom to make a copy of a recipe (given in single- or double-page format), glue it to a folder, and then laminate all sides. Open the folder so it will stand alone, allowing easy reading by the children.

Although some recipes need no cooking, others call for a hot plate, which means a common cooking time for the entire class will be requred so that the children can be supervised. For many recipes, the teacher will need to precut the ingredients so the children are not handling knives. Store the precut ingredients in Ziplock bags so that every child is assured of sufficient food when he/she has a turn at the cooking station. (One child can be the "chef" for the day to keep needed supplies restocked, to answer questions or give assistance if needed, and to be sure that each cooking group leaves the station clean for the next.)

The Little Pigs' First Cookbook
written and illustrated by N. Cameron Watson (1987)

This simple book contains bright pictures with one, two, or three sentences per page. It is an excellent example on which a child can pattern a similar cookbook. The three little pig brothers—Charles, Bertram, and Ralph—are just learning to cook. Their menus for breakfast, lunch, dinner, and dessert are interspersed throughout the story. Many of the menus require simple cooking, but there are several that don't, such as yogurt and cereal. The breakfast menus particularly are good for classroom cooking. Personal Pancakes are made by spooning out the batter with a soup spoon onto a griddle or frying pan to form the shapes of letters. The recipe also shows the batter being ladled out for pancakes. Children can create their own menus or similar stories that include menus with food that they particularly enjoy eating and cooking.

Book Cooks: Literature-Based Classroom Cooking—35 Recipes for Favorite Books Grades K–3
by Janet Bruno (1991), illustrated by Raquel E. Herrera

If you can buy only one cookbook, this should be the one! It is very simple with little cooking required for many recipes, and it stresses connections to literature, math, reading, physical and chemical changes in science, and other areas of the curriculum. The table of contents lists the books connected with each recipe for easy access. In addition to "10 Easy Steps for a Successful Book Cook Experience" and "Helpful Hints" (that remind teachers to check for children's food allergies, to delete or substitute foods according to students' preferences, etc.), there are hints for managing classroom cooking and setting up a cooking center; suggestions for using parent volunteers; and sections on kitchen math, safety, and parent letter forms. The recipes themselves are in double-page formats so you could glue copies onto a folder and laminate them to provide a self-standing recipe. The recipes are simple, inexpensive, and fun. I usually have the children write about the book and the cooking experience in their favorite format. We share the cooking, the literature, and their write-ups, all of which I try to photograph in action!

Cookie Fun
by Judith Hoffman Corwin (1985)

Cookie Fun is a wonderful cookbook to use with children. The only regret I have is that this excellent resource is out of print, but I strongly recommend trying to find a copy from one of the out-of-print resources listed in Appendix B or from your school or municipal library or one of the libraries listed in Appendix J.

Features I like include:

- Simple, large illustrations (provides ideas for illustrating children's own recipes)

- Table of contents (provides easy access to recipes listed by holidays)

- Bear Code (rates level of difficulty of recipes on a "bear scale" of one, two, or three bears—three bears require the most patience and time)

- A Few Words for Beginning Bakers (tips such as having an adult's help and permission to use the kitchen, rolling out and cutting the dough, checking oven temperatures and times, using metal spatulas to remove cookies immediately after baking, and turning off the oven and stove-top dials when finished cooking)

- Starting to Bake (reading recipes from beginning to end before starting, checking to see that all ingredients and equipment are available before beginning, washing hands before cooking, following recipes exactly, cleaning up after cooking, inviting family and friends to share, and storing leftover cookies in airtight containers)

- Cooking Utensils (what is needed to make cookies)

- The "Basic Cookie" Recipe (ingredients, materials needed, and directions for making basic cookie dough and colored or chocolate icing for rolled cookies)

- Recipe Bears (pattern for paper "recipe bear" to accompany cookies that are given to a friend, providing a place for writing out the recipe for the cookie gift; also good page format for writing about making cookies in class)

This cookbook is helpful in connecting holidays and classroom cooking. One of my favorite recipes in the book combines cooking and art and is called Stained Glass Cookies. These are prepared in class and baked in the lunchroom. When you make Stained Glass Cookies, follow the recipe exactly as it is given. Basically, it calls for lining cookie sheets with aluminum foil, preparing the dough and rolling it out to ¼" thickness, cutting the dough into very simple 3" shapes, cutting out a 1" square in the center of each, and filling the opening with crushed hard candies before baking. As a follow-up, we sometimes make Stained Glass Candy from my mother's recipe (see Appendix K).

I let the children decide how they will write about making cookies. Some choose to write about the process itself (sequence); some write a story about our class cooking experience to post in the hall; some create a story about what happens to the cookies when they are given to other people; others write about which senses they used in making them. After we've made and written about Stained Glass Cookies (or Stained Glass Candy), we do research about artists who work with real stained glass and look for pictures to share with each other.

Kids' Multicultural Cookbook: Food & Fun Around the World
by Deanna F. Cook (1995), illustrated by Michael P. Kline

This book tells children that "cooking is a fun way to learn about cultures around the world" (page 5) and gives them some good tips to think about before they start cooking. Author Deanna Cook, who has been to all parts of the world, shares recipes for the foods she has eaten and information about the children she has met during her travels. The book contains more than 75 recipes, as well as games and details about cultural traditions and customs from around the world. The recipes are given with clear, step-by-step directions and call for ingredients found in most grocery stores. My favorite parts include:

- Let's Get Cooking! (basic kitchen rules before beginning to cook)

- Easiest, Easier, Easy (recipe ratings using one spoon for the easiest recipes, two spoons for recipes that are "a little more involved, but you can do it!" and three spoons for recipes that tell the cook, "You may need a grown-up to help you with these" [page 7])

- Measuring Up (measuring liquid and dry ingredients)

- All Mixed Up (definitions with pictures for common cooking terms, such as "blend," "stir," "mix," "whisk," "strain," "beat," "sift," "whip")

- Stove-Top Cooking (cautions children to never use the oven, stove, or microwave without the help of a grown-up, and uses pictures and words to explain common terms such as "boil," "sauté," "simmer," "melt," "broil," and "toast." Kitchen safety tips include asking for help when boiling water and smothering a pan fire by turning off the heat and covering the pan with its lid.)

- Baking Basics (discussions of pictured terms: "grease," "dust," "roll," and "cool"; safety tips for using pot holders when handling anything hot)

- Microwave Cooking (reminders for children to ask a grown-up for help when using a microwave and to use only microwave-safe dishes, never metal or foil)

Using this book provides an excellent way to introduce other cultures to the classroom and to celebrate the diversity of families or neighbors. I invite children to bring a guest to talk to us about the background culture of their family and the foods they eat, and to include a sample of the food for us to taste if possible. We then write about our favorites and what we learned about the different cultures, and make a class book as a follow-up to our multicultural tasting parties. Sometimes we prepare a recipe from the book as a class cooking project.

Everybody Cooks Rice
by Norah Dooley (1991), illustrated by Peter J. Thornton

This last book shows children that even though we have many differences and come from various cultures, we do have things in common. One is the fact that many cultures include rice in their diet. In this picture book, children see ethnicities and ages portrayed appropriately throughout its pages. The story opens with a young girl, Carrie, reading. Her mom, who is cooking dinner, asks her to find her little brother, Anthony, and call him in to eat.

The girl goes from door to door in their neighborhood, trying to find Anthony. Because it is dinnertime, the families are all preparing or eating dinner. Mr. and Mrs. Darlington, from Barbados, have their grandchildren over to eat black-eyed peas and rice. Not finding Anthony, Carrie goes to the Diaz family's home, where her friend and her friend's little brother are cooking dinner because their mom is working late. They are having a meal that their Puerto Rican grandmother taught them to make: rice and pigeon peas. Next she goes to see Dong Tran, whose family came from Vietnam five years earlier. The Tran family takes turns cooking; this evening it is Dong's turn to prepare fried rice with peas. At Rajit Krishnamurthy's house they are having an Indian dish called *biryani*, made of peas, cashews, raisins, lots of spices, and a special rice called *basmati*. Not finding Anthony, she visits the Huas family, who came from China last year. They will use chopsticks to eat the rice they are steaming and the tofu and vegetables they are cooking in the wok. Carrie moves on to check for Anthony at the home of the Bleu family. She finds them having a Creole-style Haitian dinner with hot peppers, chives, red beans, and rice. Finally, she gets tired of searching for Anthony and returns home. In the kitchen she finds him showing a kitten to their baby sister, Anna, as their mother prepares *risi e bisi*, a recipe her grandmother from northern Italy gave her. This dish also includes rice, plus green peas with butter, grated cheese, and nutmeg.

Carrie found out that *everybody* cooks rice . . . and she loves it! Recipes are given for the meal of each family mentioned in this delightful book. We use it to create rice dishes and our own books about other things that people of different cultures have in common.

By allowing children's experiences to lead their writing, we teachers offer our students many advantages:

- They are able to easily find a topic.

- They are often quite motivated to write because they know a great deal about the topic from personal experience.

- They are interested in sharing with an audience and in listening to what others have to say about the same topic, thus becoming aware of the importance of writing for an audience and of the connection between writing and reading/listening.

- They have many varied and authentic purposes for writing in multiple genres and formats.

- They view learning, sharing, writing, and reading as meaningful, important, and fun!

The concluding figures in this chapter—reflections about Elsewhere Expeditions—demonstrate the importance that children attach to their experiences (see Figures 22–23 on pages 133–134).

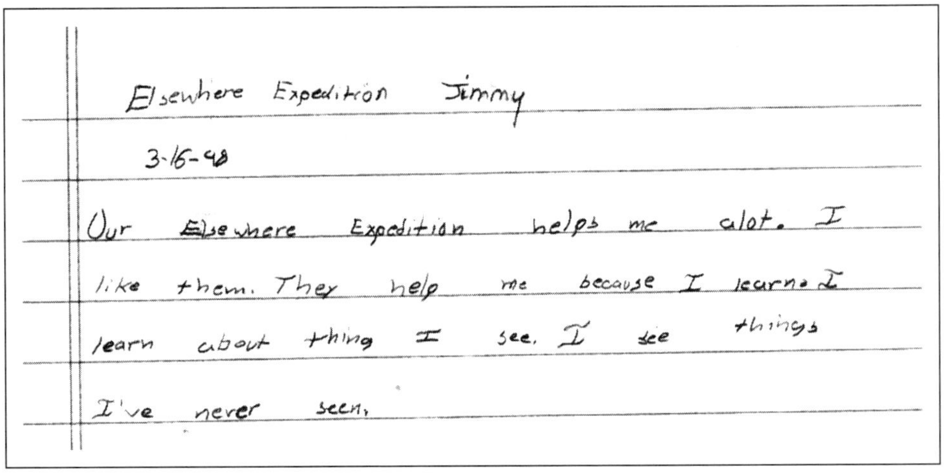

> Elsewhere Expedition   Jimmy
>
> 3-16-98
>
> Our Elsewhere Expedition helps me alot. I
> like them. They help me because I learn. I
> learn about thing I see. I see things
> I've never seen.

Figure 22. Jimmy's (top) and James's (bottom) reflections on the importance of Elsewhere Expeditions

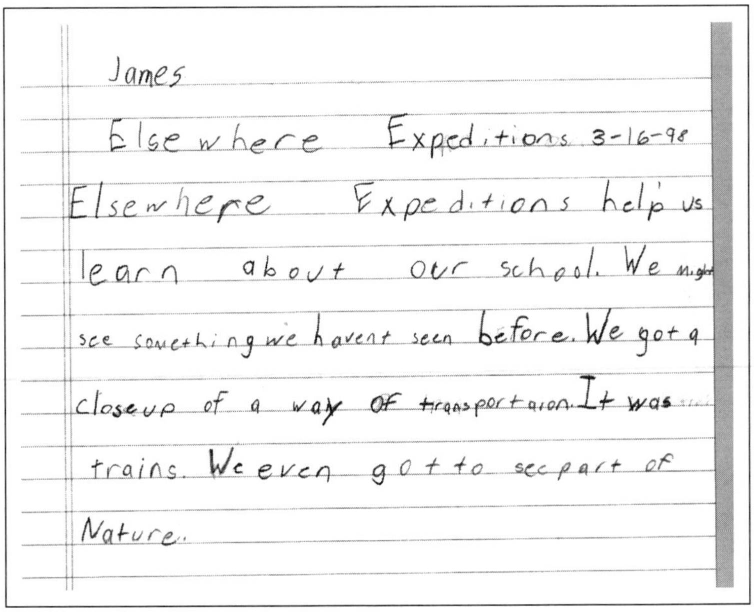

> James
>
> Elsewhere Expeditions 3-16-98
>
> Elsewhere Expeditions help us
> learn about our school. We might
> see something we havent seen before. We got a
> closeup of a way of transportaion. It was
> trains. We even got to sec part of
> Nature.

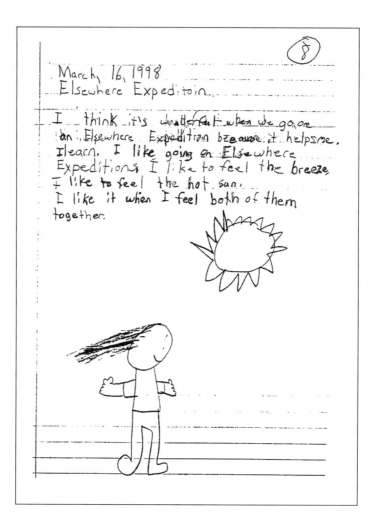

Figure 23. Jessica's
enthusiastic reflections on
Elsewhere Expeditions

CHAPTER 6

A BALANCING ACT: LITERACY ACROSS THE CURRICULUM

This last chapter is all about balance—the many kinds of balance required of teachers every day in every classroom. It discusses balancing philosophical considerations and administrative edicts within a practical format, balancing curriculum considerations, balancing time constraints, making writing conferences manageable, and making ongoing assessment an integral part of the literacy process. Then, like pulling closed a drawstring bag, I bring the book to its conclusion with a section on "Reminders for Teachers of Young Children."

BALANCING PHILOSOPHICAL CONSIDERATIONS WITHIN A PRACTICAL FORMAT

One of the most important areas to consider when designing and carrying out classroom instruction is the philosophy on which the classroom is built. During my years of teaching, I have developed a deep and abiding belief in certain ways of working with children, especially *young* children.

I believe in a constructivist philosophy of learning. I do not see children as "empty vessels" into which I "pour" knowledge. I see them as learners who build upon their prior experience, who work hard to "come to know" about the world around them, who create layers of meaning as they dialogue with peers (and me) about the phenomena they are experiencing, and who work best in their "zone of proximal development"— explained by Vygotsky (1978) as:

> . . . the distance between the actual developmental level as determined by individual problem solving and the level of potential development as determined through problem solving

under adult guidance or in collaboration with more capable peers. . . . The zone of proximal development defines those functions that have not yet matured but are in the process of maturation, functions that will mature tomorrow but are currently in an embryonic state. These functions could be termed the "buds" or "flowers" of development rather than the "fruits" of development (page 86).

I want the students in my classes to be working just ahead of where they would be able to work by themselves; therefore, I strive to set up circumstances to accommodate this. I allow the children to talk softly at many times of the day about what they are doing and what they are learning. This is not to say that there are not times that children need to work independently without talking, but I make sure that there are *many* opportunities for them to talk with others about their work. I also structure the classroom in such a way that children can work interactively and cooperatively, as I believe that literacy is a complex process that is interactive and interpretative, the development of which is determined by the cultural and social context in which it occurs (Bruner 1966, Luria 1981, Vygotsky 1978).

I also believe in *scaffolding* children as they learn. This idea is based on Bruner's (1966) work, which was further described by Wood, Bruner, and Ross (1976) as a support system that helps children gain success with tasks that would be too difficult for them to accomplish alone. I particularly like Rogoff's (1990) idea of children as being *apprentices* who acquire diverse knowledge and skills under the support and guidance of more knowledgeable people. Dorn, French, and Jones (1998) speak of structuring classrooms toward this apprenticeship model, in which teachers provide "adjustable and self-destructing scaffolds" (page 17) that are available as long as children need them and are removed when they are no longer necessary.

The ideas I have presented in this book have worked as adjustable, collapsible scaffolds for my own students. I have worked hard to discover which philosophical ideas and theories have been most helpful to the students in my classrooms over the years. I have struggled to find a workable, practical balance that allows me to put my philosophical beliefs into practice within a classroom that is imperfect and fluid, adjusting the circumstances every year to meet the needs of the students at that time.

When I first began moving from the primarily behaviorist stance of my undergraduate education of 30-odd years ago toward the more constructivist stance of my graduate work, accomplished over the intervening years, I found myself almost constantly experiencing inner cognitive conflict—"disequilibrium," as Piaget (1977) might term it. I was trying to assimilate what I was learning about children and their learning into what I had long believed and practiced. I had considered myself a good teacher for all of the years I had been teaching—yet, at this late stage, I was discovering other ways of teaching that I believed were better for children. I was frustrated and unhappy because I was unable to mesh the two philosophies. I first tried to "balance" my classroom by using half of one philosophy and half of the other. I used constructivist methodologies and tried to manage them within a behavioristic system of control.

That way of teaching simply did not work for me. What eventually happened was that I began to modify my classroom philosophy to accommodate what I was learning and what I had intuitively picked up during those many years of working closely with children. I found myself changing the ways I managed my classroom. It moved from being a silent, still place in which I "poured out" my lessons into what I had thought were "waiting vessels," and it became an active, exciting place where the children and I learned from each other, sharing what we found. No longer was the classroom silent and still. It was busy with the hum of engaged learners working together to move forward in our learning. I gave up being in total control. I allowed children many more choices and a voice in the decisions that affected us all. I still worked very hard—perhaps harder than ever before—but I was working in new and different ways (see Stewart 2000 for a description of these). The main thing I did was to totally incorporate Cambourne's previously mentioned conditions of learning— immersion, demonstration, expectations, responsibility, use, approximations, response, and engagement (Brown and Cambourne 1987, page 26)—into my teaching. This change was not an easy process. In fact, my teaching was a work-in-progress . . . and remains so today.

My goal in designing a literacy learning environment is to provide children with Cambourne's conditions. I believe in immersing classrooms in print, making available a variety of books and trying to include both a constantly changing element of literature to ensure excitement and a steadily constant core of literature to encourage reflection and re-enjoyment of favorites. I believe in involving children with books, reading to them often and having them read to me and to each other at every available opportunity. I believe in having children write regularly in as many formats and for as many purposes as possible. I believe that allowing children to connect with books by becoming authors themselves unlocks a whole new perspective for those who may never have thought about print as being the way someone is sharing thoughts with them. I think sharing the warmth, humor, comfort, and excitement of books is one of the greatest gifts we can give our students!

I have come to believe in these essential ways of working with children, no matter who they are or what their situations: love them, look for the good in them, accept them as they are, encourage them to give their best, allow them choices, and appreciate their approximations toward their goals. I believe with Delpit (1988) that it is our responsibility to make explicit the rules and conventions of the culture of power to all students, and with McLaren (1989) that we must start our practice with the problems and needs of our students in the effort to keep from marginalizing *any* of our children.

I believe that we teachers learn from our students, gaining understandings that enrich our lives and make each new day exciting and filled with possibilities. By accepting students as individuals, unique and important in their own right, we may unlock a realm of opportunities for success in the classroom. I believe we should be—and should encourage our students to be—accepting without displaying a negative devaluing of efforts, thereby building a risk-free environment in which students can thrive and grow.

As I put these ways of teaching into practice, even my principal and coworkers noticed the difference. As I gained expertise in managing my classroom in these new and exciting ways, in providing experiences for my students that moved each individual forward, and in involving children in responsible decision making and self-reflective assessment, my classroom became a place in which all of us worked productively and happily together. This is not to say that I never again experienced problems and the normal headaches of classroom living. I did and still do.

In a nutshell, what makes the difference for me and for the children is the way we think of ourselves as *co-learners* and supportive members of a bonded classroom family. There is *joy* in our classroom . . . and that joy makes all the difference!

Balancing Administrative Edicts within a Practical Format

One of the most difficult aspects of schooling is balancing what administrators and others outside the immediate classroom think should be done within it with what teachers and others inside the classroom believe is most useful. Young teachers, particularly, come out of their university classrooms wanting to save every child and to turn around the problems and difficulties of education. They are usually confident that they know what should be done and that they can do it. Very quickly these new teachers are bombarded with the "real world" in which they must deal with many situations and circumstances beyond their control. Sadly, many times they are urged by more experienced teachers or their administrators to "forget what you learned in college—that stuff just doesn't work. You have to go back to the basics and get control of your class. Your new ideas just won't work in this setting."

I think that attitude hurts all of us. We *need* the freshness and fire of new teachers with their enthusiasm for helping children learn. What all of us *must* do is remember why we got into teaching in the first place— because we love children and want to help them learn. Then we have to search our hearts and minds to find what we believe is best for them . . . and *do* it. It has been my experience that administrators usually back teachers who are successful with their students. (Sometimes other teachers are not supportive of those who want to try new ideas, but they often "come around" over time as they see the students' excitement, engaged learning, and success.) I suggest inviting your administrators to your classroom, involving them with the children, telling them what you are doing—and *why*. Then you should probably prepare to receive a roomful of children who need your "special" way of working!

I am reminded of a new principal at one of the schools where I taught. When she first started, she wanted all of her elementary faculty to follow the central administration's edicts about how to use our new literature basal. We were to follow the teacher's manual exactly, reading every story in order and working on every minute skill through drill-and-practice charts and workbooks. She told us to teach all of our children through whole-group lessons. Although we told her that not all of our children could read "on grade level," she was sure that the district's reading plan would work well for our students. She said that she expected such lessons to be on our lesson plans and when she came into our classrooms to observe she expected to see those same lessons in progress.

I approached her very early in her first year there to tell her what I did with my children and to ask that she allow me to continue doing so. She was not familiar with me or with my ways of working with children. She told me in no uncertain terms that she wanted me to follow the plan she had presented in our faculty meeting. I tried. I did try. But it just did not work for me or for my children, so many of whom were already far behind in the areas of reading and writing, even though they were only second graders.

What I then did was learn to "balance" my principal's expectations with what I felt was right for these children. I learned to read the stories from the literature basal to the whole class. They were excellent stories. I really liked them and thought they were good for children. But very few of my students could read at second-grade level. I went to the municipal library and checked out "real" books—trade book versions of the stories in our literature basal. I brought in these trade books and read them to the children so they would know they were "real" books by "real" authors, illustrated by "real" artists. I encouraged the children to follow along in their literature basals, reading what they could, looking at the pictures, and listening to the meaning of the story. I encouraged them to look for differences between what was in their text and what was in the trade book version I was reading aloud. I left the library books in the classroom for the two weeks that they were ours. (I kept them on the chalk tray and in a special laundry basket so that we would not get them mixed up with other books. I taught students how to care for library books and how to be responsible for keeping all of them in the basket or on the chalk tray so that we would not lose any before the time to return them to the library.) The combination of these practices helped elevate the lessons from being only basal-bound to becoming meaningful interactions with real books and a practical application of the advantages of checking out books from the library.

I translated skill lessons given in the charts and workbooks to more authentic contexts. I embedded the skills in whole pieces of connected text, and then pulled them out for examination and use, finally putting them back into whole pieces of connected text as the children wrote and read meaningful stories, using the skills they had learned. I used the skill books in a different way. I saved the workbooks for times I had substitutes, many of whom were much more comfortable with that format of instruction and class management. I allowed children to take workbook pages home when parents clamored for extra homework or work for the summer. But I made sure that parents and substitutes alike knew that I felt that real reading and real writing were the most important aspects of children's literacy learning.

Back to the story of my principal. I decided that if she really *knew* what the children were doing, she would probably like it. So every time we were doing a project, we invited her to come to see it in all stages of development. The children were such enthusiastic learners that she couldn't help noticing, and I became aware, too, that she dropped by unannounced more often. The children would go up to her, take her by the hand, and bring her over to their work, often telling her to listen to what they were reading or to something that they had written.

Eventually, my principal came to trust me as a teacher. She knew that my students and I were engaged in real learning. She knew that we were neither quiet nor still, but she could tell that our noise and movement were productive and that the children were engaged in self-extending learning.

Today she is one of the true leaders of her state in supporting literacy in her school, district, and beyond. She reads widely in the professional literature, attends professional conferences regularly, and has become an inveterate "kidwatcher."

The moral of this story is that as teachers we should find what we believe is best for our students, work hard to teach in those good ways, and share the excitement and success we enjoy with those who make decisions that affect us, so that they will be aware of the consequences of their decisions, as well as the possibilities for learning and engagement that they may never before have considered.

BALANCING CURRICULUM CONSIDERATIONS

Curriculum is a critical area of consideration in schools. Not only must teachers teach what their students need to learn in order to be successful at a particular grade level, but they must also find ways to teach everything mandated from school, district, state, and national levels. Sometimes those mandates are explicit, as in the case of memos from principals, supervisors, or superintendents or of state curriculum guidelines or mandated standards and benchmarks. Sometimes the mandates are implicit, as in the case of suggested areas of study in preparation for high-stakes or other norm-referenced testing. Whatever the source, teachers must include in their planned curriculum many subject areas as required by many sources. Because more and more is mandated for teachers to accomplish within the same amount of existing time, teachers must become adept at scheduling, juggling, and integrating content areas in new and effective ways.

As I entered a new grade level, a new school, or a new state, I found it helpful to obtain copies of all mandates concerning curriculum as soon as possible. Then I looked for ways they overlapped, making myself a list of the specifics given. I looked for logical ways to "chunk" those aspects of curriculum so that I could combine them to bring greater depth to my instruction and more meaning to the children's learning. Over the years, I learned to spread my curriculum less widely and to work at a much deeper level. I decided that, for me, it made sense to teach reading, writing, language, and math through science, social studies, literature, music, art, drama, and physical activity. As technology came into those mandates from above, I learned to integrate it meaningfully into my ongoing good instruction. I found ways to purposefully use cameras, tape recorders, computers, and video cameras to make our lessons more meaningful. I did not use those enhancements just for the sake of using them. I used them because they often helped get the content across to students in better ways.

I taught children to read and write fiction and nonfiction. I set up my classroom to make use of every minute of our school day—from the large scheduled blocks of content time to the small minutes we spent in lining up or waiting for scheduled events. I used every transition minute that I could by finding ways to pack in a quick review or hint about some content area that we were studying. Some of those transition times were fun and playful, some were serious, but all made good use of those brief moments that can easily be squandered if we are not careful.

We teachers have a responsibility to decide how to fit the content of schooling to our children, not the other way around. We look at what the system tells us we must teach, we look at how our children are telling us they learn, and we find logical ways to fit the curriculum to the needs of our students.

Balancing Time Constraints

As teachers we must give children the time and opportunity to practice literate behaviors. I can remember that as a very young teacher, one of the constant sources of frustration for me was trying to find enough time in the school day to "squeeze in" all of the required subjects in a meaningful way. In the middle years of my teaching, I struggled with documenting inclusion of the mandated number of requisite minutes of instruction per subject area. I was troubled by the fact that the "powers that be" seemed always to be adding to the daily requirements and never removing anything from our teaching overload. Then, somewhere during those middle years, I stumbled upon a way to change my classroom to meet the needs of my children while also meeting my responsibilities to the local, system, and state administrators. By logically integrating content areas and "chunking" skills and content in such a way that our time made sense, children became free to learn literacy behaviors in authentic ways as we explored real, meaningful content. We learned science and social studies as we took Elsewhere Expeditions. We came back to class and talked, wrote, and read about those E.E.'s. We used the camera to document science experiments, and then created books to share what we discovered with others. We worked in teams to read good literature, to write "parallel" stories, and to create books of our own. We found ourselves involving math and reading and writing in many aspects of our days together. We tried to make good use of our time, using every extra minute to read, write, or share our work. We made learning our top priority and consciously tried to help each other focus on using our time wisely. By shifting and squeezing and molding our days, we were able to extend reading, writing, and oral language into meaningful blocks across our integrated curriculum. We had time to practice and enjoy real reading, real writing, and real talk about real interests. (See Appendix C , page 169, for a typical flexible schedule.) I purposely made our classroom blocks of time large and flexible so that logical, meaningful instruction could occur in connected chunks throughout each day and across the many weeks and months we worked together.

Making Writing Conferences Manageable

One of the main reasons many teachers give for not writing on a daily basis with their students is that the management of the process is too difficult. I also thought that when I first began using the writing process in my classroom. However, in the beginning, I decided that I valued that process enough to work through the difficulties in learning how to implement it. I encourage you to start slowly, to develop with your students classroom management routines that work in your situation, and to keep the writing process predictable and consistent. By that, I mean structure your routines so that the children know what to expect every day. They should anticipate writing so they are able to plan in advance, so they will know they can count on productive writing time every day, and so they know how to use predictable, consistent conferences to support their writing.

I have a "quick check" after the daily mini-lesson so the children can let me know how they will be spending their time (see Appendix C, Quick Check form). I keep this form on my clipboard, and at the end of the day's writing session, I look to see whether the students' writing has really followed the plan they originally made. I hold them accountable for what they say they will do. They can change their plans but they must tell me first. This keeps them more focused during writing time and less likely to sit around not knowing what to do.

At the beginning of each day's writing workshop, I usually have a mini-lesson on a topic that many students are finding difficult or one that I anticipate they will soon need in their writing. I gather the students on the area rug in the center of the room for this, which lasts about 10 minutes. Afterwards, we take time to do a "quick check," and then the students go to various places in the room to write. Having read from one group of writing folders the previous night, I know which children of that group need the first conferences. It is understood that these "folder conferences," as I call them, precede "board conferences," or the ones that the children sign up for themselves. The board conference sign-up space is simply a box drawn with chalk on the board, labeled "Writing Conferences," followed by a numbered set of about 10 blank lines. As the children feel that they need to conference with me, they write their names on the first available blank line. After I conference with them, I have them erase their names as they leave my side, and I call the next child whose name is on the list. I keep a permanent, ongoing list of conferences on my clipboard as a ready reference.

We keep the rotating list of names on the board so the children can see when they have an upcoming turn. It helps them remain patient as they wait for a conference. They understand that while they are waiting, they may do things such as continue writing on their current piece, begin a new piece, read over another piece in their folder, go to a peer to have a peer conference, or read someone else's writing (or a book) to get new ideas for their own writing. These are the only activities that I allow because I want the writing time to be relatively quiet and very productive. I have found that when I let children work in centers during this time, writers often become distracted and the entire writing workshop can become less focused and meaningful. I no longer have centers in operation during writing or reading workshops.

By keeping writing a predictable daily routine, children learn to anticipate this time. By keeping writing conferences predictable, students learn to model their peer conferences on good conferencing techniques. By being consistent in setting expectations for writing, in holding writing workshops and conferences, and in allowing time to share written pieces, the teacher helps students learn to predict, plan for, emulate, and attend to important aspects of their writing.

Making Ongoing Assessment an Integral Part of the Process

Ongoing assessment is a sometimes-overlooked aspect of literacy instruction. In this day of attention to high-stakes testing, teachers are pressured to "cover" the material on which the students will be tested. This sometimes results in teachers attending to formal testing at the expense of daily instruction in writing, which is a most powerful factor in building children's facility with reading, vocabulary, spelling, and other conventions of language, as well as in building expertise in writing itself. What is ironic (and often overlooked) is that daily instruction also often brings about higher scores on high-stakes testing simply because through writing, students become more expert at reading, interpreting, and responding to tests, just as they do to any other printed matter. By writing *to* children every day, writing and thinking aloud *with* them every day, and having *them* write and share their writing every day, teachers do more to prepare children for high-stakes testing than with any other one type of instruction they can provide! A real aid to writing comes in the form of ongoing assessment. This means assessment over time—not a "one-shot" diagnosis of a timed and often "commanded" piece of writing done at one specific point in time. That one-shot evaluation does tell some things about a child's writing, but it does not provide the window into that child's processing and thinking that *ongoing* assessment of writing affords.

It is extremely important that standardized testing is not the only type of assessment given to children as they are learning to read and write. Assessment that is embedded as an integral aspect of instruction is crucial for developing writers to their fullest potential. Informal assessment, such as reading and taking anecdotal notes about journal writing or other informal writing, helps teachers remain constantly aware of their students' progress over time, guiding teachers in knowing what teaching points to stress and how best to scaffold their students' learning. (See Appendix H for an example of an informal assessment.)

Teachers who encourage children to work with them in selecting pieces of their writing to include in portfolios and who discuss the reasons for selection with their students, encouraging self-reflection and self-assessment about reading and writing, are helping those students grow into more productive and more capable writers and users of language. If students see their teachers assessing their own writing as they model writing and thinking aloud, the students learn to incorporate those same practices into their own thinking and writing. Students learn to think about what is good in their writing, what could be better, how they can change it to make it stronger, and how to make those changes by using proofreading marks and editing strategies.

Reminders for Teachers of Young Children

As teachers we must affirm children's strengths.

Possibly the most fulfilling aspect of teaching comes as teachers affirm children's strengths. Since I have realized the power of this mechanism in the classroom, I look for opportunities to practice it. When I went back to school in the late 1980s, I realized the impact that acceptance of approximations, teacher response, and affirmation can have on students. As a student myself, I was curious about what I did well, where I needed to improve, and what my teachers and peers thought of my work. As I reflected upon the impact those processes had for me, I learned to apply them more consistently as I work with children. Written feedback is crucial. Personal comments written on a paper in support of some insightful commentary by a student—whether a second grader or a graduate student—result in greater attention being paid to that point.

When working with students of any age, I often request that they allow me to make overhead transparencies of their work to share with their peers. I point out every good thing I find (e.g., strong ideas, good story lines, meaningful sequences, unusual interpretations, strong punctuation, good capitalization, etc., depending upon the ages of the students involved) and focus the attention of the class on those strengths. I am careful to point out one area of needed improvement so that the students' learning might be extended as they work to become stronger writers. I think it is important to find just one area on which the student should focus for the next assignment. It is essential that teachers not overwhelm students by mentioning every error in their work at one time. The most effective strategy in my own classrooms has been to share with each student (most often from the overhead) all the good things, point out one thing to think about for the next time they write, and to do this consistently over time. Then each child in the class hears specific "good things," each child hears the specific teaching point targeted at a particular error, and all try to incorporate both the "good things" and the teaching point in their own work. Considering the number of days available in the school year, addressing one specific point per day (multiplied by the number of children who share on a daily basis) yields a tremendous number of specific, relevant, and remembered teaching points. This really works!

I feel that it is very important to accept children's approximations on their way toward using conventions of language. With young children I find that this approach to learning through students' strengths is especially helpful in calling attention to strong approximations in spelling, causing children to risk spellings of which they are unsure as they stretch their processing abilities to accommodate their rapidly expanding vocabularies. Quite early each year, using dictionaries with peer support becomes an integral part of the editing process for these young students, once they have captured their thoughts on paper and are preparing to share them.

Another positive outcome of this approach to learning through student strengths is that *all* of my students quickly see themselves as "smart." *All* are learners, capable of producing good things in their work, and all have ideas worthy of being shared with their peers. Not only do the students see themselves as capable learners, but their peers (and I) do also. Perhaps this sharing of positive elements of student work—thus also a sharing of the students themselves as learners—is the most powerful factor in changing our classrooms from being a collection of separate individuals to becoming a bonded, caring community of friends. We support each other in our learning experiences, finding that our shared literacy experiences extend and enrich our lives across our year together.

As teachers we must teach children to make responsible choices.

One of the things that really makes a difference with children (and with older students, for that matter) is that they are given many opportunities to make choices in their daily schooling experience. By giving students choices and requiring them to be responsible for those choices, the tone of my classroom changes remarkably. No longer am I the only person who has an investment in what goes on in our classroom. As children give input and take charge of choosing appropriate ways to learn, they also become invested in that learning. What *they* decide is significant in their assignments takes on added importance for them. Their work takes on a more serious tone. I move from settling squabbles and helping students refocus their attention on the task at hand to facilitating and supporting meaningful learning experiences. The children spend their time more productively. Their work increases in merit. Those constant elements of personal choice make a definite contribution to the quality of our classroom and to our relationships with each other. To be more specific, I try to give children many choices—in seating, in work settings (i.e., with partners, in groups, or as individuals), and in assignments. If it is not feasible to give choices in the entire assignment, I try to include at least some element of choice in carrying out the assignment or in the order of completing given assignments, etc. Children have frequent opportunities to self-select texts; to choose subjects, genres, and formats for their writing; and to choose modes of presenting finished investigations. We experience a wide range of plays, murals, poetry, buildings, costumes, songs, books, and other projects as children share their work with the group. We applaud each other. We learn from each other. We enjoy each other as we explore our choices for learning.

As teachers we must create classrooms that focus on learning— especially literacy learning—as an enjoyable activity.

Throughout my years of working with young children, I have found that when the children enjoy their learning, they are more involved in it and engage in it more often. Current literature in the field of early literacy supports this statement (see, for example, McQuillan 1998; Snow, Burns, & Griffin 1998; Weaver 1998).

If we want our children to become good thinkers, readers, writers, and speakers, we must help them learn to find joy in those experiences. Children who enjoy literacy activities tend to engage in them and become stronger readers and writers. Children who engage in reading and writing for pleasure tend to become children who *stay* readers and writers for life. And after all, isn't that exactly what we're trying to achieve with our children?

A Parting Thought—Keys for Successful Writing Experiences with Young Children:

- Trust your knowledge about children.

- Start *now*, where you *are*, and begin to grow by *doing*.
  ("Plant thy feet in mid-air and proceed."—Gary Manning)

- Be *observers* of children.
  ("Kidwatchers."—Yetta Goodman)

(*continued*)

- *Listen* to children.

- Be willing to give the children control over their writing.

- Help your students view themselves as *real authors*.

- Be a writer *yourself*. (Experience the joys and frustrations firsthand.)

- *Model* good writing in front of children.

- Be willing to *think aloud* with children so they will experience with you the thought processes that accompany writing efforts.

- Allow sufficient *time* for writing *every day*.

- Be *consistent* in your scheduling of writing.
  (*Predictable scheduling* allows children to *plan ahead*.)

- Be *consistent* in your expectations for writing.
  (*Predictable expectations* allow children to *internalize* those expectations [Calkins 1983, page 137].)

- Be *consistent* in your conferencing about writing.
  (*Predictable conferencing* allows children to pattern peer conferences on good teacher conferences. [Calkins 1983, page 139].)

- Be *consistent* in having students *share* their writing with a *real audience*.
  (*Predictable sharing* leads children to *predict responses* of real audiences and, later, to internalize those audiences. [Calkins 1983, page 61].)

- Focus on *everything good* in your students' writing.

- After pointing out strengths, comment on *only one* area of needed improvement. As students gain confidence you may sometimes wish to point out two such areas. Once a safe, caring community has been established, you may wish to invite peer critiques.

- *Write with* your children. *Share yourself* with your children through your own stories.

- Let your students *see* that you enjoy them and their writing!

WORKS CITED

Allard, Harry. *The Stupids Die*. Boston: Houghton Mifflin, 1981.

Allard, Harry, and James Marshall. *The Stupids Have a Ball*. Boston: Houghton Mifflin, 1978.

Allington, Richard L., and Patricia M. Cunningham. *Schools That Work: Where All Children Read and Write*. New York: Longman, 1996.

Amoss, Berthe. *Cajun Gingerbread Boy*. New Orleans: MTC Press/More Than a Card, 1999.

_____. *A Cajun Little Red Riding Hood*. New Orleans: MTC Press/More Than a Card, 2000.

Atwell, Nancie. *Coming to Know: Writing to Learn in the Middle Grades*. Portsmouth, NH: Heinemann, 1990.

Baker, Augusta. *The Black Experience in Children's Books*. New York: New York Public Library, 1984.

Baltas, Joyce, and Susan Shafer, eds. *Scholastic Guide to Balanced Reading K–2: Making It Work for You*. New York: Scholastic Professional Books, 1996.

Baylor, Byrd. *The Desert Is Theirs*. New York: Charles Scribner's Sons, 1975.

_____. *Hawk, I'm Your Brother*. New York: Charles Scribner's Sons, 1976.

_____. *I'm in Charge of Celebrations*. New York: Charles Scribner's Sons, 1986.

_____. *The Table Where Rich People Sit*. New York: Charles Scribner's Sons, 1994.

_____. *The Way to Start a Day*. New York: Charles Scribner's Sons, 1978.

_____. *Your Own Best Secret Place*. New York: Charles Scribner's Sons, 1979.

Benson, Vicki, and Carrice Cummins. *The Power of Retelling: Developmental Steps for Building Comprehension*. Bothell, WA: The Wright Group, 2000.

Brett, Jan. *Goldilocks and the Three Bears*. New York: Troll, 1987.

Brown, Hazel, and Brian Cambourne. *Read and Retell: A Strategy for the Whole-Language/Natural Learning Classroom*. Portsmouth, NH: Heinemann, 1987.

Brown, Marcia. *Stone Soup: An Old Tale*. New York, Charles Scribner's Sons, 1947 (renewed 1975).

Bruner, Jerome S. *Studies in Cognitive Growth: A Collaboration at the Center for Cognitive Growth*. New York: Wiley, 1966.

Bruno, Janet. *Book Cooks: Literature-Based Classroom Cooking—35 Recipes for Favorite Books Grades K–3*. Cypress, CA: Creative Teaching Press, 1991.

Calkins, Lucy McCormick. *The Art of Teaching Writing*. Portsmouth, NH: Heinemann, 1986.

_____. *Lessons from a Child: On the Teaching and Learning of Writing*. Portsmouth, NH: Heinemann, 1983.

Calkins, Lucy McCormick, and Shelly Harwayne. *The Writing Workshop: A World of Difference*. Portsmouth, NH: Heinemann, 1987.

Cambourne, Brian, and Jan Turbill. *Coping with Chaos*. Rozelle NSW, Australia: Primary English Teaching Association, 1987.

Carle, Eric. *The Very Hungry Caterpillar*. New York: Philomel Books, 1981.

Cole, Joanna. *Golly Gump Swallowed a Fly*. New York: Parents Magazine Press, 1981.

Cook, Deanna F. *Kids' Multicultural Cookbook: Food & Fun Around the World*. Charlotte, VT: Williamson Publishing, 1995.

Corwin, Judith Hoffman. *Cookie Fun*. New York: Julian Messner, 1985.

Cullen, Esther. *Spiders*. New York: MONDO Publishing, 1986.

Cunningham, Patricia M., and Richard L. Allington. *Classrooms That Work: They Can All Read and Write*. 2nd ed. New York: Longman, 1999.

Delpit, Lisa D. "The Silenced Dialogue: Power and Pedagogy in Educating Other People's Children." *Harvard Educational Review* 58 (1988): 280-298.

dePaola, Tomie. *The Legend of the Poinsettia*. New York: G. P. Putnam's Sons, 1994.

_____. *Pancakes for Breakfast*. New York: Harcourt Brace, 1990.

_____. *The Popcorn Book*. New York: Holiday House, 1978.

Dooley, Norah. *Everybody Cooks Rice*. Minneapolis, MN: Carolrhoda Books, 1991.

Dorn, Linda J., Cathy French, and Tammy Jones. *Apprenticeship in Literacy: Transitions Across Reading and Writing*. York, ME: Stenhouse, 1998.

Dorn, Linda J., and Carla Soffos. *Scaffolding Young Writers: A Writers' Workshop Approach*. Portland, ME: Stenhouse, 2001.

Dorros, Arthur. *Ant Cities*. New York: HarperCollins, 1987.

Ferreiro, Emilia, and Ana Teberosky. *Literacy Before Schooling*. Portsmouth, NH: Heinemann, 1979.

Fletcher, Ralph. *What a Writer Needs*. Portsmouth, NH: Heinemann, 1993.

Fletcher, Ralph, and JoAnn Portalupi. *Craft Lessons: Teaching Writing K–8*. Portland, ME: Stenhouse, 1998.

Flournoy, Valerie. *The Patchwork Quilt*. New York: Dial Books for Young Readers, 1985.

Fox, Mem. *Memories: An Autobiography*. Flinders Park, South Australia: Era Publications, 1992.

Ghigna, Charles. *Tickle Day: Poems from Father Goose.* New York: Hyperion Books for Children, 1994.

Giff, Patricia Reilly. *Next Year I'll Be Special.* New York: Delacorte Press, 1980a.

_____. *Today Was a Terrible Day.* New York: Puffin Books, 1980b.

Goodman, Yetta M. "Kidwatching: Observing Children in the Classroom." In *Observing the Language Learner.* Edited by Angela Jaggar and M. Trika Smith-Burke. Newark, DE: International Reading Association and Urbana, IL: National Council of Teachers of English, 1985.

Graves, Donald H. *A Fresh Look at Writing.* Portsmouth, NH: Heinemann, 1994.

_____. *Writing: Teachers and Children at Work.* Portsmouth, NH: Heinemann, 1983.

Greenfield, Eloise. *Grandpa's Face.* New York: Philomel Books, 1988.

_____. *Honey, I Love.* New York: HarperFestival, 1978.

_____. *Honey, I Love and Other Love Poems.* New York: Harper Trophy, 1972.

_____. *She Come Bringing Me That Little Baby Girl.* Philadelphia: J. B. Lippincott, 1974.

Hansen, Jane, and Donald Graves. "The Author's Chair." *Language Arts* 60 (1983): 176–183.

Harnadek, Anita. *Mind Benders: Deductive Thinking Skills.* Pacific Grove, CA: Critical Thinking Books & Software, 1978.

Hillert, Margaret. *What Am I?* Chicago: Follett, 1981.

Houston, Gloria. *Littlejim's Gift: An Appalachian Christmas Story.* New York: Philomel Books, 1994.

Huck, Charlotte S., Susan Hepler, Janet Hickman, and Barbara Z. Kiefer. *Children's Literature in the Elementary School.* 6th ed. Boston: McGraw Hill, 1997.

Kasza, Keiko. *The Wolf's Chicken Stew.* New York: G. P. Putnam's Sons, 1987.

Keats, Ezra Jack. *John Henry: An American Legend.* New York: Scholastic, 1987.

Kellogg, Steven. *Paul Bunyan.* New York: Morrow, 1986a.

_____. *Pecos Bill.* New York: Scholastic, 1986b.

Lester, Julius. *John Henry.* New York: Dial, 1994.

Luria, Alexander R. *Language and Cognition.* Edited by James V. Wertsch. New York: Wiley, 1981.

McCarrier, Andrea, Gay Su Pinnell, and Irene C. Fountas. *Interactive Writing: How Language & Literacy Come Together, K–2.* Portsmouth, NH: Heinemann, 2001.

McLaren, Peter. *Life in Schools: An Introduction to Critical Pedagogy in the Foundations of Education.* New York: Longman, 1989.

McQuillan, Jeff. *The Literacy Crisis: False Claims, Real Solutions.* Portsmouth, NH: Heinemann, 1998.

Manning, Maryann Murphy, Gary L. Manning, Roberta Long, and Bernice J. Wolfson. *Reading and Writing in the Primary Grades*. Washington, DC: National Education Association 1987.

Merrilees, Cindy, and Pamela Haack. *Write on Target: Practical Advice from Real Teachers*. Peterborough, NH: Crystal Springs Books, 1990.

Moustafa, Margaret. *Beyond Traditional Phonics: Research Discoveries and Reading Instruction*. Portsmouth, NH: Heinemann, 1997.

_____. "Whole-to-Parts Phonics Instruction." In *Practicing What We Know: Informed Reading Instruction*. Edited by Constance Weaver. Urbana, IL: National Council of Teachers of English, 1998.

Mr. Know-It-Owl's Video School: All About Animals. Produced by Michael Wright and directed/edited by Hamid Naderi. 48 min. Apollo Educational Video. Videocassette. 1986.

Mwalimu. "Awful Aardvark." In *All Kinds of Friends*. Edited by Roger C. Farr and Dorothy S. Strickland (Sr. Authors). Orlando: Harcourt Brace, 1995.

Mwalimu, and Adrienne Kennaway. *Awful Aardvark*. Boston: Little, Brown, 1989.

National Research Council. *Starting Out Right: A Guide to Promoting Children's Reading Success*. Edited by M. Susan Burns, Peg Griffin, and Catherine E. Snow. Washington, DC: National Academy Press, 1999.

Noble, Trina Hakes. *The Day Jimmy's Boa Ate the Wash*. New York: Dial, 1980.

Norris, Janet A. Guest lecture, "Strategies for At-Risk Learners," presented to the author's graduate class, Louisiana State University, Baton Rouge, LA, 2 February, 1999.

Numeroff, Laura Joffe. *If You Give a Moose a Muffin*. New York: Scholastic, 1991.

_____. *If You Give a Mouse a Cookie*. New York: Harper & Row, 1985.

Numeroff, Laura, and Felicia Bond. *Mouse Cookies: 10 Easy-to-Make Cookie Recipes with a Story in Pictures*. New York: HarperFestival, 1995.

Ogle, Donna M. "K-W-L: A Teaching Model that Develops Active Reading of Expository Text." *The Reading Teacher* 39 (1986): 564-570.

Parrish, Peggy. *Amelia Bedelia*. New York: Harper & Row, 1963.

Peterson, Ralph. *Life in a Crowded Place: Making a Learning Community*. Portsmouth, NH: Heinemann, 1992.

Pfister, Marcus. *The Rainbow Fish*. Translated by J. Alison James. New York: North-South Books, 1992.

Piaget, Jean. *The Development of Thought: Equilibration of Cognitive Structures*. New York: Viking Press, 1977.

Pilkey, Dav. *The Paperboy*. New York: Orchard Books, 1996.

Pinkney, Sandra L. *Shades of Black: A Celebration of Our Children*. New York: Scholastic, 2000.

Polacco, Patricia. *My Rotten Redheaded Older Brother*. New York: Simon & Schuster Books for Young Readers, 1994.

_____. *Thunder Cake*. New York: Philomel Books, 1990.

Portalupi, JoAnn, and Ralph Fletcher. *Nonfiction Craft Lessons: Teaching Information Writing K–8*. Portland, ME: Stenhouse, 2001.

Pretlutsky, Jack. *Read-Aloud Rhymes for the Very Young*. New York: Alfred A. Knopf, 1986.

Ralph, Judy, and Ray Gompf. *The Peanut Butter Cookbook for Kids*. New York: Hyperion Books, 1995.

Rogoff, Barbara. *Apprenticeship in Thinking: Cognitive Development in Social Contexts*. New York: Oxford University Press, 1990.

Routman, Regie. *Conversations: Strategies for Teaching, Learning, and Evaluating*. Portsmouth, NH: Heinemann, 2000.

_____. *Invitations: Changing as Teachers and Learners K–12*. Portsmouth, NH: Heinemann. 1994.

San Souci, Robert D. *The Talking Eggs: A Folktale from the American South*. New York: Dial Books for Young Readers, 1989.

Sendak, Maurice. *Where the Wild Things Are*. New York: Harper Trophy, 1984.

Silverstein, Shel. *A Light in the Attic*. New York: HarperCollins, 1981.

_____. *Falling Up*. New York: HarperCollins, 1996.

_____. *The Giving Tree*. New York: HarperCollins, 1964.

_____. *Where the Sidewalk Ends*. New York: HarperCollins, 1974.

Sims, Rudine. *Shadow and Substance: Afro-American Experience in Contemporary Children's Fiction*. Urbana, IL: National Council of Teachers of English, 1982.

Snow, Catherine E., M. Susan Burns, and Peg Griffin, eds. *Preventing Reading Difficulties in Young Children*. Washington, DC: National Academy Press, 1998.

Stead, Tony. *Is That a Fact? Teaching Nonfiction Writing K–3*. Portland, ME: Stenhouse, 2002.

Stewart, Margaret Taylor. *"Best Practice"? Insights on Literacy Instruction from an Elementary Classroom*. Newark, DE: International Reading Association, and Chicago, IL: National Reading Conference, in press.

Stewart, Margaret. "A View from the Threshold." *Reading: Exploration and Discovery (R.E.A.D.)* 20 (2) (2000): 13-22.

Strickland, Dorothy S. *Teaching Phonics Today: A Primer for Educators*. Newark, DE: International Reading Association, 1998.

Strickland, Dorothy S., and Lesley Mandel Morrow, eds. *Beginning Reading and Writing*. New York: Teachers College, and Newark, DE: International Reading Association, 2000.

Sutton, Wendy K., ed., and the Committee to Revise the Elementary School Booklist. *Adventuring with Books: A Booklist for Pre-K–Grade 6.* 11th ed. Urbana, IL: National Council of Teachers of English, 1997.

Trelease, Jim. *The Read-Aloud Handbook.* 4th ed. New York: Penguin Books, 1995.

_____. *The New Read-Aloud Handbook.* New York: Penguin, 1989.

Viorst, Judith. *Alexander and the Terrible, Horrible, No Good, Very Bad Day.* New York: Aladdin Books, 1972.

Vygotsky, L. S. *Mind in Society: The Development of Higher Psychological Processes.* Edited by M. Cole, V. John-Steiner, S. Scribner, & E. Souberman. Cambridge, MA: Harvard University Press, 1978.

Wagstaff, Janiel M. *Teaching Reading and Writing with Word Walls: Easy Lessons and Fresh Ideas for Creating Interactive Word Walls that Build Literacy Skills.* New York: Scholastic Professional Books, 1999.

Watson, N. Cameron. *The Little Pigs' First Cookbook.* Boston: Little, Brown, 1987.

Weaver, Constance, ed. *Reconsidering a Balanced Approach to Reading.* Urbana, IL: National Council of Teachers of English, 1998.

Williams, Vera B. *"More, More, More," Said the Baby: 3 Love Stories.* New York: A Mulberry Paperback Book, 1990.

Wood, D., J. Bruner, and G. Ross. "The Role of Tutoring in Problem Solving." *Journal of Child Psychology and Psychiatry* 17 (2) (1976): 89–100.

Young, Ed. *Lon Po Po: A Red Riding Hood Story from China.* New York: Philomel, 1989.

APPENDIXES

VIRGINIA'S DRAWSTRING BAG PATTERN

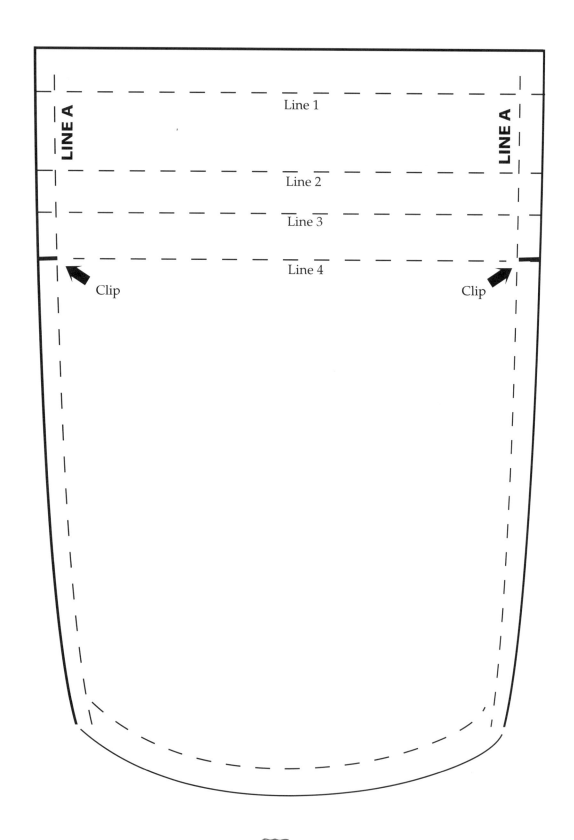

DIRECTIONS:

1. Enlarge or widen the pattern as desired.

2. With right sides of the fabric together, cut out the pattern on double thickness of fabric. Use nonpermanent ink or wax-free sewing tracing paper to transfer pattern markings to fabric. Mark lines A, 1, 2, 3, and 4 on both sides of the fabric as shown on the pattern.

3. Make the upper casing for the cords (or ribbons or string) as follows, repeating the steps for the other piece of fabric:

   a. On line 4 make a ⅜″ cut on both edges of the fabric as shown on the pattern.

   b. Starting at the cut and working toward the top of the bag, turn this side edge under by ⅜″ (**along line A**) to the wrong side of the fabric. Press.

   c. Hem both upper side edges to form a finished edge for the casing.

   d. Turn the top edge of the bag under (**along line 1**) to the wrong side of the fabric. Press.

   e. Turn the pressed edge under again, to the wrong side of the fabric, so it aligns with **line 4**. Pin in place and stitch just above and parallel to line 4 to reinforce the edge. Stitch along **line 3** to form the casing and the upper ruffle of the bag.

4. Bag body:

   a. With right sides of the fabric together, pin both pieces together along the outside edges. Stitch a ⅜″ seam along line A, starting below line 4 (below casing) and continuing down the side, around the bottom, and up the opposite side, ending just below the casing (below line 4). Be sure not to stitch over the ends of the casing, where the cords will be inserted.

   b. Turn right-side-out and press. You now have a bag with a ruffled top edge and a casing for the cords.

(continued)

5. Cords:

   a. Cut 2 cords (or ribbons or string), both to a length that is 2½ times the width of the bag.

   b. Run 1 cord through the casing on both sides of the bag, going all the way around the bag, so that both ends of the cord come out on the same side of the bag. (It is helpful to temporarily fasten a safety pin to the leading end of the cord before attempting to feed it through the casing.)

   c. Repeat this step with the other cord, entering and exiting from the opposite side of the bag.

6. Knot both ends of the cords together so they will not slip through when the bag is opened.

7. To draw the bag closed, hold the 2 cords on one side of the bag with one hand and the 2 cords on the other side of the bag with the other hand, and pull. You have successfully closed the bag!

RESOURCES

Sources for Further Information About Writing

There are many excellent sources to refer to about teaching writing in the classroom. If you can purchase only one book, however, I suggest *A Fresh Look at Writing*, by Donald Graves. There are several earlier works that I also recommend, such as *Writing: Teachers and Children at Work*, also by Graves; *The Art of Teaching Writing*, by Lucy Calkins; and *Interactive Writing: How Language & Literacy Come Together, K–2*, by Andrea McCarrier, Gay Su Pinnell, and Irene Fountas. Other good references include *Coming to Know: Writing to Learn in the Middle Grades*, by Nancie Atwell, which has implications for earlier grades as well; "The Author's Chair," by Jane Hansen and Donald Graves; and *What a Writer Needs*, by Ralph Fletcher. A book that gives many insights into the writing process is *Lessons from a Child* by Lucy Calkins.

For a more practical, less theoretical view of writing, I recommend *Write on Target: Practical Advice from Real Teachers*, by Cindy Merrilees and Pamela Haack. This little book gives writing ideas in a monthly format for times when teachers need a way to "jump-start" their young authors who say they have nothing to write. I do not suggest following the format precisely, but many of the ideas do lend themselves well to early childhood classrooms of very young authors. Pick and choose those that you feel will integrate easily into your own classroom situation.

Complete citations for recommended resources follow:

Allington, Richard L., and Patricia M. Cunningham. *Schools That Work: Where All Children Read and Write*. New York: Longman, 1996.

Atwell, Nancie. *Coming to Know: Writing to Learn in the Middle Grades*. Portsmouth, NH: Heinemann, 1990.

Calkins, Lucy McCormick. *The Art of Teaching Writing*. Portsmouth, NH: Heinemann, 1986.

_____. *Lessons from a Child: On the Teaching and Learning of Writing*. Portsmouth, NH: Heinemann, 1983.

Calkins, Lucy McCormick, and Shelly Harwayne. *The Writing Workshop: A World of Difference*. Portsmouth, NH: Heinemann, 1987.

Cambourne, Brian, and Jan Turbill. *Coping with Chaos*. Rozelle, Australia: Primary English Teaching Association, 1987.

Cunningham, Patricia M., and Richard L. Allington. *Classrooms That Work: They Can All Read and Write*. 2nd ed. New York: Longman, 1999.

Dorn, Linda J., Cathy French, and Tammy Jones. *Apprenticeship in Literacy: Transitions Across Reading and Writing*. York, ME: Stenhouse, 1998.

Dorn, Linda J., and Carla Soffos. *Scaffolding Young Writers: A Writers' Workshop Approach*. Portland, ME: Stenhouse, 2001.

Fletcher, Ralph. *What a Writer Needs*. Portsmouth, NH: Heinemann, 1993.

Fletcher, Ralph, and JoAnn Portalupi. *Craft Lessons: Teaching Writing K–8*. Portland, ME: Stenhouse, 1998.

Graves, Donald H. *A Fresh Look at Writing*. Portsmouth, NH: Heinemann, 1994.

——————. *Writing: Teachers and Children at Work*. Portsmouth, NH: Heinemann, 1983.

Hansen, Jane, and Donald Graves. "The Author's Chair." *Language Arts* 60 (1983): 176–183.

McCarrier, Andrea, Gay Su Pinnell, and Irene C. Fountas. *Interactive Writing: How Language & Literacy Come Together, K–2*. Portsmouth, NH: Heinemann, 2001.

Manning, Maryann Murphy, Gary L. Manning, Roberta Long, and Bernice J. Wolfson. *Reading and Writing in the Primary Grades*. Washington, DC: National Education Association, 1987.

Merrilees, Cindy, and Pamela Haack. *Write on Target: Practical Advice from Real Teachers*. Peterborough, NH: Crystal Springs Books, 1990.

Portalupi, JoAnn, and Ralph Fletcher. *Nonfiction Craft Lessons: Teaching Information Writing K–8*. Portland, ME: Stenhouse, 2001.

Stead, Tony. *Is That a Fact? Teaching Nonfiction Writing K–3*. Portland, ME: Stenhouse, 2002.

Strickland, Dorothy S., and Lesley Mandel Morrow, eds. *Beginning Reading and Writing*. New York: Teachers College, and Newark, DE: International Reading Association, 2000.

Wagstaff, Janiel M. *Teaching Reading and Writing with Word Walls: Easy Lessons and Fresh Ideas for Creating Interactive Word Walls that Build Literacy Skills*. New York: Scholastic Professional Books, 1999.

CHECKOUT AND PURCHASING INFORMATION

MR. KNOW-IT-OWL'S SCHOOL—ALL ABOUT ANIMALS
Available for library checkout:

Original videocassette: *Mr. Know-It-Owl's Video School: All About Animals.*

Produced by Michael Wright and directed/edited by Hamid Naderi. 48 min. Apollo Educational Video, Van Nuys, CA, 1986, videocassette (ISBN: 0-8068-7051-6).

I have been unable to purchase this original videocassette, but it is available for checkout from various school and municipal libraries. I go to the Sheraden Branch **http://www.einpgh.org/clp/SH/** then click on "Sheraden's multimedia." This takes me to "Old Video List." I click on that to find "Mr. Know-It -Owl's All About Animals," available for checkout.

This source has the title listed as "*Mr. Know-It-Owl* [videorecording]: *All About Animals.*" The author is listed as United American Video. Published in Charlotte, NC: United American Video, 1992, c1991. Music Pub no.: 5278 United American Video. System ID no.: AGB-1707. This video is listed as (item #j136). A listing of other library sources can be found in Appendix J of this book.

Available for purchase:

Although I have been unable to purchase the video recently, I have found it in CD-ROM format. Each of the five CDs included in the AIMS Multimedia production contains a video clip from the original video. Some labels are flashed on the screen as in the original. This is a usable format for getting across note taking for young children. The least expensive source I have found of the CD-ROM is "Videos for Kids," Schoolmasters Video, 745 State Circle, Box 1941, Ann Arbor, MI 48106. The item number is CD180W28, available for $59.95 plus shipping and handling. This description comes from the Schoolmasters web site: "Mr. Know-It-Owl's™ All About Animals—This informative program introduces children to the amazing world of mammals, birds, reptiles, amphibians, and fish . . . Over 30 minutes of curriculum video, beautiful still shots, and educational fact cards illustrate physical and behavioral characteristics as well as some unusual features of animals . . . Upbeat educational songs and engaging activities . . . Grades K–6 . . . Mac/Win compatible." **http://school-tech.com/cdrom7a.html**

- Aims Multimedia products may be accessed directly at 9710 DeSoto Avenue, Chatsworth, CA 91311-4409; telephone: 1-800-367-2467; fax: 818-341-6700; or via the Internet at **http://www.aims-multimedia.com**

BARE BOOKS

Available from Treetop Publishing, P.O. Box 085567, Racine, WI 53408-5567; call 1-800-255-9228; e-mail **treetop@execpc.com**; or fax 262-884-0700 to order or to request a catalog and price list. Information is also on the World Wide Web, available at **http://www.barebooks.com** for those preferring to use the convenience of a web site.

LOGIC PROBLEMS

As mentioned in the text, a good source of logic problems is *Mind Benders: Deductive Thinking Skills* by Harnadek (1978), published by Critical Thinking Books & Software. To request their catalog or to place an order, you can write the company at P. O. Box 448, Pacific Grove, CA 93950-0448, call 1-800-458-4849 or 831-393-3288; fax 831-393-3277; or e-mail **ct@criticalthinking.com.** The information is available at **http://www.criticalthinking.com/** for those who prefer the convenience of a web site.

OUT-OF-PRINT RESOURCES

There are several good sources for locating out-of-print books and other resources, including the following:

- "ByTheBooks.com" **http://www.bythebooks.com/**
  (Directs user to Amazon.com, Alibris, Barnes & Noble, half.com, Varsity Books, Borders Books)

- "AddALL Used and Out of Print search" **http://www.addall.com/used/**
  (Advertises searches at 40 bookstores; 20,000 dealers; options for these stores: ABE Books, Alibris, Antiqubook, Bibliofind, Biblion, Elephantbooks, half.com, ILAB, JustBooks.co.uk, JustBooks.de, Powell's Books)

- "Used Books Online" **http://www.used-book-dealers.com/**
  (Gives brief commentary and links to Alibris, Powell's Books, Elephant Books, half.com, and eBay)

I have had extremely good luck with:

- "Amazon.com" **http://www.amazon.com**

- "Barnes & Noble" **http://www.barnesandnoble.com**

- "Searchbiblio.com" **http://www.biblio.com**

When all else fails, I try "Dogpile" metasearch engine (using search terms "out of print"). This metasearch engine searches multiple search engines and invariably finds excellent results.

http://www.dogpile.com

SAMPLE CLASSROOM FORMS

"Quick Check" Class Record Sheet Showing Choices During Typical Writing Workshop

I attach this record sheet to my clipboard and use it as a "quick check" to record choices made by the students before they begin writing in each day's writing workshop. I write each student's name beside his or her ID number (names in alphabetical order which are then numbered; this helps student "captains" record various types of information to keep our classroom running smoothly) and make copies with the names already in place. Then, each day, I simply write the title (or topic) of the student's writing for the day, quickly record the genre (tall tale, biography, poem, adventure, family story, etc.), and the format (flip book, bi-fold book, picture book, step book, etc.) at the beginning of our workshop. At first this took about 5 to 10 minutes, but after we settled into a routine, it required only 2 to 3 minutes. The time is well spent because the children are more focused as they begin and continue their writing. I jot a note out by the side of the numbered column if I had a conference with that child. I also record the date at the top of the page.

At the end of our writing workshop, those children who share what they have written answer the questions listed above the right-hand columns in the form: Did you actually write about what you planned? Did you stay on the subject? Did you complete your piece? Will you continue to write about this topic? Did you use your time well? Sometimes I spot-check the other students who might not have had an opportunity to share. At other times, I quickly record each child's answers to the questions as I ask them aloud of the group. This is also very brief, but helps us remain focused.

"Quick Check" Class Record Sheet

Student Number	Student Name	Title (or Topic)	Genre	Format	Did you actually write about what you planned?	Did you stay on the subject?	Did you complete your piece?	Will you continue to write about this topic?	Did you use your time well?
1									
2									
3									
4									
5									
6									
7									
8									
9									
10									
11									
12									
13									
14									
15									
16									
17									
18									
19									
20									
21									
22									
23									

RETELLING SCORE SHEET FOR "AWFUL AARDVARK" BY MWALIMU

This record sheet is one that I developed to help me record the children's retellings of "Awful Aardvark." (I modified this sheet for use with a few other stories, as well.) I was attempting to give a numerical value to the children's holistic retellings so I could use them as part of the child's writing/reading grades (mandated by my school system). I experimented with various point values for the different stories I used, depending upon the number of items I devised for that particular story. I was never totally satisfied that I had the points entirely right. I tried to adjust them according to the point in the year that I was doing the assessing, as well as to the story itself. I used whatever point value I assigned to a story for a particular time of the year with every child at that point. I was trying to get a comparison of their retelling strengths and needs at a common point in time. This was not something I did with every story. I much prefer to do a completely holistic scoring. This suggestion is made for those teachers who must give a numeric value to the assessment of their students.

RETELLING SCORE SHEET* FOR "AWFUL AARDVARK" BY MWALIMU (1995)

WRITTEN/ORAL RETELLING OF "AWFUL AARDVARK"			STUDENT'S NAME:			DATE:		
COMPREHENSION—STRENGTHS: (Each correct detail scores 5 points.)	+	Pts.	**MECHANICS—STRENGTHS:** (Score points as listed.)	+	Pts.	**GRAMMAR—STRENGTHS:** (Score points as listed.)	+	Pts.
Aardvark sleeps in tree, resting nose on smooth branch.			Title is capitalized correctly. (15 pts.)			All (15), many (10), few (5), no (0) sentences are grammatically correct.		
Aardvark's snoring keeps other animals awake. HHHRRR—ZZZZ!			All (15), many (10), few (5), no (0) sentences begin with capital letters.			All (15), many (10), few (5), no (0) verbs are used correctly.		
Mongoose is annoyed by Aardvark's snoring.			All (15), many (10), few (5), no (0) proper nouns are capitalized correctly.			All (15), many (10), few (5), no (0) nouns are used correctly.		
Aardvark only stops snoring when sun comes up, clambering down to hunt for grubs and beetles.			All (15), many (10), few (5), no (0) sentences end with correct punctuation.			All (15), many (10), few (5), no (0) subjects and verbs agree.		
Mongoose gets idea to meet with friends: Monkeys, Lion, Rhinoceros.			All (15), many (10), few (5), no (0) periods are used correctly.			All (15), many (10), few (5), no (0) correct uses of "me" / "I."		
Aardvark snores again that night.			All (15), many (10), few (5), no (0) question marks are used correctly.			Other strengths:		
Mongoose calls Monkeys, who shake Aardvark's tree.			All (15), many (10), few (5), no (0) commas are used correctly.					
Aardvark wakes up, shouting, "Stop making that noise."			All (15), many (10), few (5), no (0) quotation marks are used correctly.					
Aardvark goes back to sleep, snoring loudly.			All (15), many (10), few (5), no (0) possessives are used correctly.					
Mongoose calls Lion, who scratches bark with strong claws.			Spelling is completely conventional. (15 pts.)					
Aardvark shouts, "Stop it! Go away!" then goes to sleep, snoring loudly.			Spelling is almost conventional. (10 pts.)					
Mongoose gets angry, and his fur bristles.			Spelling is transitional. (5 pts.)					
Mongoose calls Rhinoceros, who puffs up and bumps tree with his fat bottom.			Spelling is emergent. (1 pt.)					
Munching sound comes from roots of Aardvark's tree just before tree CRACKS and topples.			All (15), many (10), few (5), no (0) spelling miscues are circled.					
Aardvark asks, "Who did that?"								
Lion, Rhinoceros, Monkeys, and Mongoose deny causing tree to fall.			MECHANICS SCORE:			GRAMMAR SCORE:		
Aardvark spots termites, threatens, then eats them as they hide in sand and mud.								
From that time to this, Aardvark slept during day and ate termites at night.								
Mongoose and other animals sleep peacefully, no longer bothered by Aardvark's awful snoring.			OTHER STRENGTHS: (20 points for each strength)			NEEDS/COMMENTS:		
			Difficult words are attempted.					
			Variations in letter size indicate volume of speech or emphasis.					
			Humor is evident.					
Details (Score)			Illustrations are included.					
Retelling is in correct sequence (Score)			Perseverance at task is evident.					
Retelling contains beginning, middle, end of story and/or problem and solution (Score)			Dedication is included with retelling.					
Retelling contains main idea of story (Score)			Author page is included with retelling.					
COMPREHENSION SCORE:			Neatness/readability					

*This was a way in which I tried to give a numerical value to my holistic scoring of retellings in order to give credit within my district's required grading system for a child's progress in authentic writing.

Sample second-Grade Schedule with Large "Chunks" of Integrated Teaching Time

7:45–10:40	LANGUAGE ARTS BLOCK
	(READING, WRITING, SPELLING, SPEAKING, LISTENING)

	7:45–8:00	Journals (M., W., F.)/Other Writing Formats (T., Th.)
	8:00–8:15	Class Meeting
	8:15–9:30	Reading Workshop
	9:30–10:40	Writing Workshop

10:40–11:05	LUNCH
11:05–11:15	READ ALOUD (Special Favorite or Chapter from Chapter Book)
11:15–11:30	D.E.A.R. Time (Drop Everything and Read!)
11:30–12:30	MATH
12:30–1:00	PHYSICAL EDUCATION
1:00–1:30	READ ALOUD (Often connected to unit. Children eat snacks during this time if they wish.)
1:30–2:30	INTEGRATED UNIT AND SKILLS:
	LANGUAGE, SPELLING, SOCIAL STUDIES, SCIENCE, HEALTH, FINE ARTS
2:30–2:45	CLASS MEETING (Daily reflections/discussions/problem solving/planning)
2:45	PREPARE TO GO HOME
2:50	DISMISS CAR RIDERS/WALKERS
2:55	DISMISS BUS RIDERS

STORY COMPARISON MATRIX FOR COMPARING DIFFERENT VERSIONS OF THE SAME STORY OR RETELLING

I use this story comparison as discussed in Chapters 4 and 5, comparing two different versions of tall tales, different versions of two culture's retellings of the same folktale or fairy tale, or two children's versions of the same experience. This form also serves well when comparing a trade book version of a story to a literature basal version, or a video version to a book version. Versatile and practical, it can be used similarly to ways I use Venn diagrams. I like it also for the specificity it suggests to children.

Name _____ Date _____

Partner or Group _____

Comparison Matrix

Version 1	Version 2
Title	
Author	
Illustrator	
Similarities	
Differences	
Which story do you like best?	Why do you like it?
If you were creating another version of this story, what are three things you would do differently? Why?	
1.	Reason:
2.	Reason:
3.	Reason:

WHOLE-GROUP AND SMALL-GROUP CHART STORIES

"NUTSHELL" VERSION OF CREATING WHOLE-GROUP STORIES BASED ON CHILDREN'S INTERESTS

MATERIALS:

- Large chart paper (24" x 32")

- Dark, water-based marker(s)

- ¼ or ½ sheet of 8 ½" x 11" photocopier paper for each child for illustrations

CLASSROOM ORGANIZATION HINT:

When the teacher is acting as scribe for the students, it is helpful to have each child working on an individual illustration for the story. This gives the students a way to be actively involved while waiting for a turn to share an idea about the story.

By keeping the illustrations small, all may be fitted on or around the story. Encourage children to fill all the space on their illustration sheets and to make them as colorful as possible. Students write their names neatly on the back or bottom of their drawings so their illustrations are recognized as personal contributions to the story.

PROCEDURE:

Ask: "What would you like to write about today?"

Children suggest topics.

Teacher lists those topics on the board.

Children vote to choose topic for that day's group story.

Ask: "Who would like to start our story? Remember, we need a way to get our readers interested in what we are talking about so that they will really understand our subject."

Ask for someone to give the next sentence and so on. Guide the flow to promote sense; to stay on the subject; to have a logical beginning, middle, and end to the story; to have a sensible sequence of events, etc. Periodically reread the story aloud or have one of the students do so in order to keep the "sense" of the story.

As the story progresses to the end of the page, warn the students that they are running out of space and need to draw their story to an end. Remind them that they can't just stop. They must bring their story to a close, like drawing the strings of a bag to close it.

REMINDER:

It is important to add "Written and Illustrated by . . ." (the name of the class, the school, and the date) at the top or bottom of the story.

"Nutshell" Version of Creating Small-Group Stories based on Children's Interests

MATERIALS:

- Large chart paper (24" x 32")
- Dark, water-based marker(s)
- ¼ or ½ sheet of 8½" x 11" photocopier paper for each child for illustrations

CLASSROOM ORGANIZATION HINT:

Before writing, give each child ¼ or ½ sheet of illustration paper so that he or she will be able to stay focused on the task at hand during the entire time. This allows the children to make a personal contribution to the story while helping them stay calm. (Often children become very excited about their story and have a difficult time waiting for their turn to add to it.)

COMPOSITION HINT:

Remind children that writing should be like a drawstring bag. Show a bag and ask them how they can choose a beginning sentence that will situate people in their story so that they will know what is happening and will want to read to find out more.

Let someone periodically "read" what the group has written so far. Keep bringing them back to the story: "Does it make sense?" "Are we sticking to our subject?" "What should come next?" "How can we bring our story to a close?" "We do not want to just stop. We need to draw our story together like closing a bag."

PROCEDURE:

- Start with a focus: "Who wants to write about _____?"
  (dolls, football, baseball, skating, cheerleading, swimming, etc.)

or

- Start with a group and vote for the topic: "Who wants to write first?"

Call four or five children to the table with you. The groups can be *heterogeneous* or *homogeneous*—there are advantages and disadvantages to each. But usually it is good to choose different children to write together so there is a different interplay of ideas and so children do not get into the habit of always depending upon the same one or two students to compose the stories. Each child should feel that he or she has a voice and that this is his/her story. *Ownership* is a key component for writing.

REMINDER:

It is important to add "Written and Illustrated by . . ." (the names of the children involved, as well as the date) at the beginning or end of the story.

COVERING AND BINDING BOOKS

Cut Con-Tact paper along dashed lines

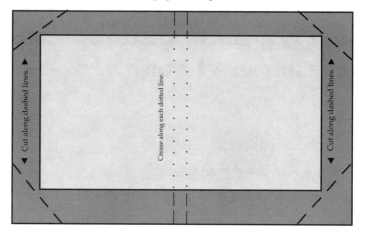

(Drawing not to scale)

Cut Con-Tact paper along dashed lines

Directions:

1. Gather five sheets of white paper for the pages, twice as long as the finished pages will be (8½"x11" photocopier paper is perfect). Cut one piece of cardboard the same size (8½"x11").

2. Cut Con-Tact paper 2" longer on all sides than the paper for the pages.

3. Place Con-Tact paper facedown (with design side down, sticky side up) on a flat surface. **Do not peel yet.**

4. Crease the cardboard in two places, making creases 1/4" apart at the center (see illustration).

5. Center the cardboard on top of the unpeeled, facedown Con-Tact paper.

6. Secure the right side of the cardboard to keep it from slipping while you peel away the Con-Tact paper, starting from the left side. Lift the cardboard to allow the peeled paper to pass under that end.

7. Press down on the left side of the cardboard as you peel away the Con-Tact paper. As you near the center, have a helper lift up the right side of the cardboard so you can continue to peel away the Con-Tact paper.

8. As the Con-Tact paper is peeled, press the cardboard firmly down onto it, beginning on the left side and working toward the right, until it is firmly and smoothly attached. Check other side and smooth out any wrinkles or bubbles.

9. Cut off the corners of the Con-Tact paper and cut along the center lines, top and bottom, to the edges of the cardboard (see dashed lines in illustration).

10. Fold over the edges of the Con-Tact paper onto the cardboard, and smooth to remove any wrinkles or bubbles.

11. Fold the white paper for the pages in half to make a center crease, and then open them out flat again.

12. Sew long stitches (by hand or machine) along the center line, or staple the pages with a long-neck stapler.

13. Spread glue over the inside of the front book cover and press the first page of the sewn pages onto the glued surface, smoothing to remove any wrinkles or bubbles. Repeat with the inside of the back book cover and last page of the sewn book pages.

14. Close the book covers, smoothing the Con-Tact paper front and back, and your book is ready for use.

STEP BOOK

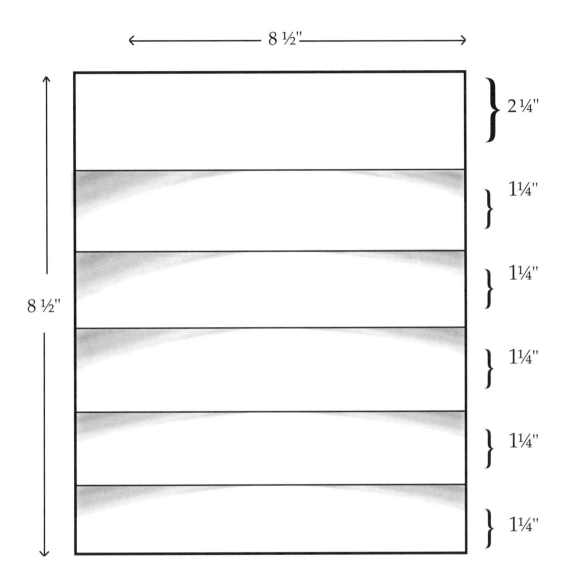

8 ½"

8 ½"

} 2¼"

} 1¼"

} 1¼"

} 1¼"

} 1¼"

} 1¼"

Directions:

1. Take three sheets of 8 ½" x 11" white paper (photocopier paper works well).

2. Stagger the sheets so that each one is approximately 1¼" above the bottom edge of the sheet below it.

3. Holding the sheets in this position, fold all three sheets over so that the top portion is also spaced in the same manner. (This makes the top flap about 2¼" wide.)

4. Staple along the top edge of the fold, creating a book consisting of six "steps." These books may be used in a variety of ways.

EXAMPLE:

JIMMY'S FIRST DAY OF SCHOOL STEP BOOK, "ALL ABOUT ME"

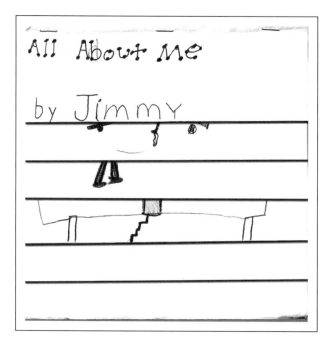

FLIP BOOK

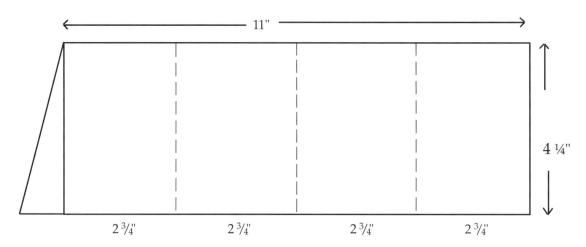

11"

4 ¼"

2 ¾"   2 ¾"   2 ¾"   2 ¾"

Directions:

1. Take a sheet of 8½" x 11" white paper (such as photocopier paper).

2. Fold it in half lengthwise so it is 4¼" wide by 11" long.

3. Cut the front only (up to the fold) at 2¾" intervals to form four separate flaps. (I usually take a stack of 3 to 4 sheets of paper, quickly fold it lengthwise, and cut through several thicknesses at the same time.)

Suggestions for use:

		Comments:
Language Arts:	"Characters, Setting, Problem, Solution"	Children may write
	"First, Next, Next, Last"	on the top flap and
Math:	"Coin Equivalents"	illustrate underneath
	"Word Problems and Solutions"	or vice versa,
Science:	"Step-by-Step Experiments"	or do both on each flap
	"Growth Stages Over Time"	as shown below.

Write name and date
on back of flip book.

Example:

HALF-PAGE JOURNAL
(MODELING CONVENTIONS OF WRITING THROUGH RESPONSIVE JOURNALING)

Directions:

1. Cut 10 sheets of blank 8½" x 11" white photocopier or lined notebook paper in half cross-wise, creating 20 sheets measuring 5½" x 8½".

2. Make a construction paper cover the same size as the paper.

3. Bind together (on the short side) the 20 half-sheet pages inside the construction paper cover (see illustration).

4. Label the cover with the child's name (and number) and the title of the journal.

5. Store journals folded back to the last page on which the student made an entry so you can simply pick up each journal, quickly read it, and respond on the corresponding page.

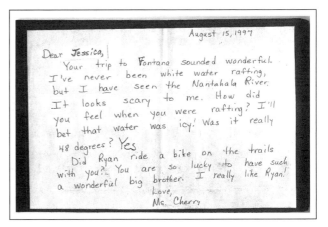

Jessica's (not her real name) first journal entry with teacher response. Note that the teacher responds by using friendly-letter format and modeling correct spelling. Also note that the teacher begins a conversation ("Was it really 48 degrees?") to which Jessica responds on the next day ("Yes"). This conversational aspect grows as time passes.

8-15-97 (from Journal entry)

Student #8 ("Jessica")

Strengths:	**Needs:**

Strengths:

+Includes element of story in her entry

+Starts sentences with capitals

+Uses a capital for the word "I"

+Ends sentences with periods

+Uses mostly conventional spelling

+Is willing to take risks in her writing:
  trales (trails), *Nannhall* (Nantahala),
  to grease (degrees)

+Has beginning, middle, and ending sounds

+Uses illustration to enhance story line

+Uses captions to expand illustration

+Is aware of abbreviations but not yet
  conventional

+Writes first and last name correctly

+Can copy date correctly in number format

Needs:

-Work on abbreviations

-Show sources for spelling: *trales* (trails),
  Nannhall (Nantahala), *to grease* (degrees)

-Work on past tense: *swum* (swam)

-Work on capitalizing city, state

-Work on proper nouns (Nantahala River)

-Work on homonyms (road/rode)

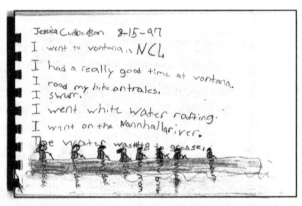

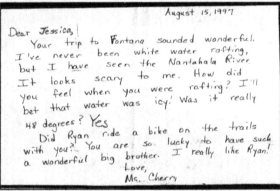

For the first few weeks, I keep a teacher's notebook listing all strengths and weaknesses I observe from the children's journaling. This is very helpful in understanding where to begin working with each child in his or her writing. I do this periodically across the year, approximately every six weeks.

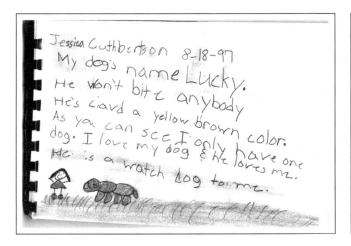

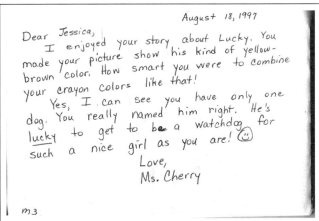

This is Jessica's second journal entry with my teacher response. Again, I am modeling correct spelling and friendly-letter format, while trying to have my response make sense. This is the way I begin to have written conversations with my students early in the year, which contributes to building not only conventional spelling, but also classroom community.

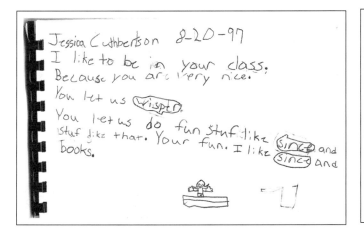

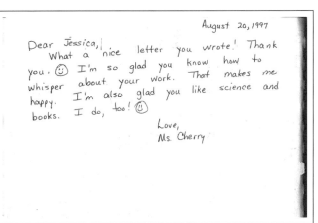

In Jessica's fourth journal entry, she begins incorporating my suggestion that she circle words that she thinks might be "spelled differently than they would be spelled in a book." (Note how close her spelling approximations are to conventional spellings!)

In my response, I model conventional spelling of "whisper" and "science" to serve as a reference for her future spellings. Also, this entry and response method continues to build a personal relationship between student and teacher as we get to know each other better through our written conversations.

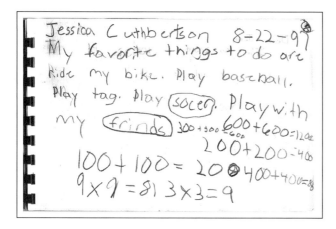

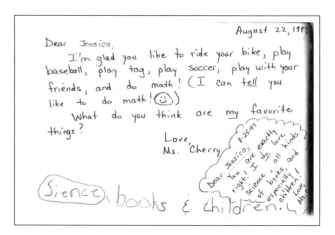

Jessica's sixth entry talks about her favorite things. (In her third entry, she spells it "favorit." Then I model correct spelling. She refers to that entry in order to spell this one correctly.) Again, she circles spelling she is unsure of, and as before, she is quite close to conventional spellings, attending well to the sounds in the words. In my response, I model correct spelling and separating items in a series with commas.

Jessica responds to my asking what she thinks are *my* favorite things by saying "science, books, and children." What a wonderful confirmation for me as a teacher!

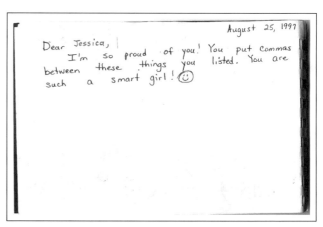

Note the influence of my sixth response (above) in which I model using commas in a series and Jessica's adoption of that correct grammatical format in this seventh journal entry. In my response to her the next day, I took time to point out to her a "good thing" from her writing. In this way, teachers can support children just as they are learning to take the "next step" in their processing.

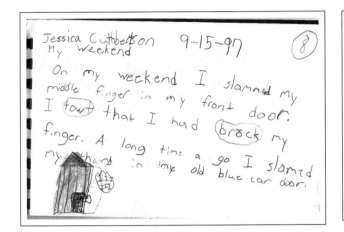
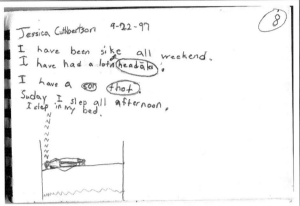

Jessica's 12th entry (left) shows her attempt to give the sounds of "broke" ("brōck," in which she uses the symbol for the "long o" sound). In her 15ᵗʰ entry (right), she continues to use symbols to help convey sounds (e.g., for "headaches" she writes "headāks," using the long "a" symbol). This child is definitely working on her spelling, demonstrating growth in each successive journal entry. (Note that she also uses a caret to insert the word "of," a revision strategy we discussed in class.)

Responsive journaling with children is an excellent way to give meaningful instruction in the mechanics of writing while also using it to build comprehension, composition, and classroom community. Although it is time-consuming for the teacher to make individual responses, it is a profitable use of the time and effort of both student and teacher. In order to keep it from becoming too much of a burden on the children or on me, I find that using responsive journaling in brief blocks of time—such as two-week periods—works well with young children.

RETELLING: AN EXAMPLE WITH COMMENTARY
MASON'S RETELLING OF JAN BRETT'S
GOLDILOCKS AND THE THREE BEARS

Please read the entire text of Mason's retelling of Jan Brett's (1987) *Goldilocks and the Three Bears*, on this and the next page, looking for the "good things" evident in his writing.

There are many reasons to do retellings with young children—in both oral and written formats. This written retelling by Mason was done four days before school was out in 1995 and shows a child who is still working, even to the end of school. Although there are certainly many errors in this retelling, if you search for conventional perfection, there also are many "good things" that indicate that Mason is a strong processor of language. His story is full of details. He uses "storybook" language that echoes the language used in the Brett text. Particularly note the beginning, as he sets the tone for his story, "Once apon ago . . ." Throughout this piece he uses language reminiscent of Brett's version of the tale. Brett uses this beginning: "Once upon a time there were three bears who lived together in a house of their own in a wood. One of them was a little, small, wee bear, and one was a middle-sized bear, and the other was a great, huge bear." Mason tells of a "tewe" (teeny weeny) bear, a "middle size" bear, and a "huge" bear. Even the picture he drew on his last page reflects Brett's illustrations of the bears (especially the depiction of the ears).

Page 1

> Goldylocks and the three bears.
> Retold by: Mason Sharp
> Once apon ago there was
> three bears one was a
> tewe little bear, then there was
> a middle size bear, and there was
> a huge bear Once when they'
> was going to ea t porage
> then it was to hot so
> they dicited to take a
> walk in the woods, Then
> there was a little girl
> named Goldylocks She was

Page 2

> Often walken in the
> woods, Then she came up
> to a house that was the
> bear's house, And she went
> in and nobody told her
> She could come in, But she went
> in anyway, And she saw
> three boles of porage, She
> tried the big bole it was too;
> hot. The second one she tried
> it. It was too cold The third,'
> she tried it she said "just right,
> Then she went and sit in
> the papa's chair. Then she went and

Page 3

> goldylocks and the three bears
>
> sit in the momas chair. Then she went and sat in the littlest chair and she rocked, and rocked til it broke CABOONK she fell on the floor. Then Goldylocks went up stairs to the beds, Then she tried the papas bed. Then she layed in the mamas bed. Then she tried little bears bed it wasn't to long or to big. Then the Bears thout their porage was cool enough.

Page 4

> then they went to there boles and started to get ^their porage! Then the papa bear said, "Some body has been eating my porage." And the moma bear also said the same thing. Then the little bear said, "somebody has been eating my porage and its all gone. And the went to their chairs. The papa bear said, "Somebody has been siting in my chair. And moma bear said, "Some body has been siting in m

Some of the strengths of this work are that Mason evidences awareness of, though he is not consistent in using, some conventions of language. Much of the time he uses periods to end sentences and capitals to begin them. He is aware of proper noun capitalization, though he uses it both correctly and incorrectly in his story. He uses a contraction with conventionally correct spelling in one instance where he attempts it (see "wasn't" on page 3, fourth line from the end) but not in the other (see "its" page 4, sixth line from the end). He uses conventional spelling in many places and strong approximations in several others (i.e., "tewe" for "teeny weeny" on page 1, "porage" for "porridge" on page 1, "decited" for "decided" on page 1, "Goldylocks" for "Goldilocks" throughout, "boles" for "bowls" on page 2, "siting" for "sitting" on pages 4–5, etc.). He tries to use quotation marks, seemingly aware of the instances of dialogue, but not exactly sure where to place the marks (notice pages 4–5). He sometimes uses "too" correctly, but is not consistent in the correct use. He uses possessives correctly in places, though not consistently. He attempts to use strong vocabulary, even when unsure of conventional spelling. He uses incorrect homonyms for some vocabulary, which shows me an area of focus for future mini-lessons. I was pleased to see Mason insert "their" using a caret on page 4, which is something we had discussed as an editing strategy.

Mason has the sense of the story and the sequence of events. He knows—and uses—all capitals to show a loud noise—"CABOONK." Though there are many instances of unconventional usage of vocabulary, spelling, and punctuation, his attention to these aspects is evident. He writes a thorough rendition of the tale— quite an accomplishment for a second grader. (Most second graders write many details for the first page or two and then seem to "wear out" before they finish writing everything they can tell aloud. Note he does take a "short cut" on his

Page 5

"chair. And the baby bear said,"
some body has been siting in
my chair and it is broken. Then
they went to their beds. The
papa bear said," some body has
been laying in my bed in his big
voice. Then the moma bear said,"
somebody has been sleeping in
my bed. Then the baby bear said,"
some body has been sleeping
in my bed and hear she is.

Page 6

fourth page: "And the moma bear also said the same thing." This makes me think that by this point, he is becoming weary of writing everything he can recall.)

However, one of the things that struck me the most as Mason shared his retelling with the class was that, even though he is a relatively strong writer, it was not until he *read* this story to the class that he recognized some of his own errors. He said, "I put two its. I was supposed to put a period right there." (He was referring to page two, fourth line from the end of that page.) He went back, grabbed his pencil, and made the correction after he read. As he continued reading to the class he said, "I left out a word again —'porridge.' " He then fixed that omission. This recognition of mistakes during shared reading is typical for young writers and is one of many valid reasons to have them share what they write with a real audience.

As with every shared writing, I point out to the child every "good thing" that I can find, which usually guarantees that those things are noticed and attempted during the next writing event. Even if the author does not consistently use the good strategy throughout the piece he or she is sharing, I point out the times he/she does. It is quite amazing how often those same correct elements will turn up in that person's future writings and in those of others in the class. I also usually point out one thing for the child to think about before the next written assignment. In this case, Mason was so close to conventional usage of quotation marks that this is what I conferenced with him about on the day of this sharing.

This retelling, with remarks about Mason's strengths and needs, describes a relatively easy way to help young children learn to write for an audience, to strive to make each piece better than the one before, and to work hard to do the best that they can do in each writing task.

CHILDREN'S LITERATURE: A GOOD PLACE TO BEGIN

CHILDREN'S LITERATURE GUIDES:

- Children's Literature Web Guide
- Commentary on Children's Books
- Essential Kid Lit Web Sites
- Readers Helping Readers
- Conference Bulletin Board
- Children's Book Awards
- Many links to other excellent sources in the area of Children's Literature
- Home page address: **http://www.acs.ucalgary.ca/~dkbrown/index.html**
- "Lots of Lists" address (including "Recommended Book Lists"):

  http://www.acs.ucalgary.ca/~dkbrown/lists.html

- American Library Association Sites for Children: Literature and Language
  http://www.ala.org/parentspage/greatsites/lit.html

  This is a wonderful site, full of exciting links!

MULTICULTURAL RESOURCES FOR CHILDREN:

- "Index to Internet Sites: Children's and Young Adults' Authors & Illustrators"
  http://falcon.jmu.edu/~ramseyil/biochildhome.htm
- "Culture, Gender, and Sexual Orientation in Children's Books"
  http://www.cynthialeitichsmith.com/newreadingb.htm

SITES FOR LOCATING INFORMATION ABOUT AUTHORS AND ILLUSTRATORS:

- "Children's Book Authors and Illustrators"
  http://www.cynthialeitichsmith.com/auth-illA-I.htm
- "Learning About the Author and Illustrator Pages"
  http://www.scils.rutgers.edu/~kvander/council3.html
- "Children's Literature Web Guide" (Authors)
  http://www.acs.ucalgary.ca/~dkbrown/authors.html
- "Interesting Personal WWW Sites of Authors and Illustrators"
  http://www.underdown.org/topsites.htm

SITES FOR LOCATING INFORMATION ABOUT FOLKLORISTS AND ARTISTS IN MANY FIELDS:

- "Louisiana Voices"   **http://www.crt.state.la.us/folklife**

- Smithsonian Institution   **http://www.pbs.org/riverofsong/artists/**
- "Swapping Stories"   **www.lpb.org/programs/swappingstories/**
- "Storytelling, Drama, Creative Dramatics, Puppetry & Readers Theatre for Children & Young Adults"   **http://falcon.jmu.edu/~ramseyil/drama.htm**

SITES FOR LOCATIONG AWARD-WINNERS AND OTHER HIGH-QUALITY BOOKS:

- The American Library Association has an outstanding web site with resources for "Parents, Teens and Kids." This page has links with other great sites, recommended readings for kids, and multimedia recommendations, as well as links for teens, parents and others, and families. This site is well worth exploring. **http://www.ala.org/parents/**

Two of those links are as follows:

Randolph Caldecott Award

The Association for Library Services to Children (a division of the American Library Association) confers this award annually to honor the illustrator of the most distinguished American picture book for children published in the United States in the year preceding the award. This award has been given since 1938. Lists may be obtained from most libraries or via the World Wide Web at **http://www.ala.org/alsc/caldecott.html**. A printable list of all Caldecott Medal Winners 1938–2000 is available at **http://www.ala.org/alsc/cquick.html**.

John Newbery Medal

The Association for Library Service to Children (a division of the American Library Association) gives this award annually for the most distinguished contributions to American literature for children. The award is given for books published in the United States in the year preceding the award. This award has been given since 1922. Lists may be obtained from most libraries or by visiting **http://www.ala.org/alsc/newbery.html**.

- *The Reading Teacher:*

    This journal is published by the International Reading Association, 800 Barksdale Road, P.O. Box 8139, Newark, DE 19714-8139. 1-800-336-READ, ext. 266. (November issues each year give "Teachers' Choices: Best New Children's Books") Available at **http://www.reading.org/** (IRA home page).

- *The New Advocate: For Those Involved with Young People and Their Literature*

    As its title indicates, this journal is dedicated to various topics concerning children's literature, including creative processes, critical issues, classroom connections, classroom vignettes, children's voices, connecting children with literature in classrooms and communities, and connecting educators with professional resources. Subscriptions may be purchased from *The New Advocate*, 1502 Providence Highway, Suite 12, Norwood, MA 02062. 781-762-5577. This is an excellent resource for teachers and teacher educators.

- Book Links: Connecting Books, Libraries, and Classrooms

    The American Library Association publishes this excellent resource every other month. It gives ideas for integrating children's books into classroom curriculum, and organizes recommended titles by reading level, grade level, genres, and themes, giving summaries of the plots and hints for incorporating

titles into specific lessons. Publisher, price, and ordering information are given. Selections are listed by topic. Subscriptions can be obtained for a reasonable rate by mailing to *Book Links*, P.O. Box 615, Mt. Morris, IL 61054.

STORYTELLING RESOURCES

- "Storytelling Resources: Storytelling" has links with organizations, events, storytellers' homepages, resources, mailing lists, and news groups interested in storytelling and children's literature. This site is "Storytelling on the Internet: Storytelling Links List" **http://www.storynet.org/resources/links.htm**

- One of the sites linked to the site above is "Children's Literature—Resources for Storytellers." This site is **http://www.ucalgary.ca/~dkbrown/rstory.html,** which is linked to "The Children's Literature Web Guide."

COMPREHENSIVE TEXTS (FAVORITE RESOURCES FOR CHILDREN'S LITERATURE)

- Huck, Charlotte S., Susan Hepler, Janet Hickman, and Barbara Z. Kiefer. *Children's Literature in the Elementary School*. 6th ed. Boston: McGraw Hill, 1997 (ISBN: 0-697-27960-X).

  This is an *outstanding* resource for school libraries. It is a good guide for teachers, parents, and librarians who purchase books for children. It includes sections entitled "Learning About Books and Children," "Exploring Children's Literature," and "Developing a Literature Program." Included in the appendixes are "Children's Book Awards," "Book Selection Aids," "Publishers' Addresses," and listings of books by name index and by subject index. Included on the front and back covers is a list of 150 books to read aloud, with recommended ages of audience.

- Routman, Regie. *Conversations: Strategies for Teaching, Learning, and Evaluating*. Portsmouth, NH: Heinemann, 2000 (ISBN: 0-325-00109-X).

  This book includes in its "The Blue Pages: Resources for Teachers" section, "Chapter 2: A Comprehensive Literacy Program: Essential Elements" (Comprehensive Literacy Resources), pp. 7b–11b; "Chapter 3: The Literature Program," pp. 11b–22b. Chapter 3 of "The Blue Pages" has resources for "The Literature Program (Fiction and Nonfiction)," "Literature Resources for Choosing Fiction and Nonfiction," "Response to Literature," "Readers Theatre," "Resources That Support Author/Illustrator Study," "Leveling Books," "Children's Magazines for the Classroom Library," and "Some Excellent K-6 Language Arts Web Sites." "Recommended Literature by Grade Level, K–8, and Supplemental Lists" with annotations by Susan Hepler, is included in pp. 74b–121b. "Supplemental Literature" is discussed with resource recommendations on pp. 122b–132b.

- Routman, Regie. *Invitations: Changing as Teachers and Learners K–12*. Portsmouth, NH: Heinemann. 1994 (ISBN: 0-435-08836-X).

  This book includes in its "The Blue Pages: Resources for Teachers" section, "Recommended Literature by Grade Level, K–12, and Supplemental Lists," pp. 103b–166b, with annotations by Susan Hepler (K–8) and Dana Noble (9–12). There is a "Multicultural Book List," pp. 167b–169b, as well as several appendixes related to children's literature. See "Appendix A: A Folk/Fairy Tale Unit for Grades 3–6," pp. 170b–185b; "Appendix B: Teacher's Guide for Amos & Boris," p. 186b; "Appendix C: Teacher's Guide for Journey to Topaz," pp. 187b–188b; and "Appendix D: Using the Goldilocks Strategy to Choose Books," p. 189b. Other worthwhile information is included.

- Sutton, Wendy, ed., and the Committee to Revise the Elementary School Booklist. *Adventuring with Books: A Booklist for Pre-K–Grade 6.* 1997 ed. Urbana, IL: National Council of Teachers of English, 1997 (ISBN: 0-8141-0080-5).

This lists books by topic with a short synopsis of each. The chapters are divided into "Books for Young Children," "Poetry," "Traditional Literature," "Fantasy," "Contemporary Realistic Fiction," "Historical Fiction," "Biography," "Social Studies," "Science: Pure and Applied," "Fine Arts," "Crafts and Hobbies," and "Celebrations: Fiction and Nonfiction." Supplementary resources are "Prizes and Lists" (which is a wonderful compendium of winners of the most prestigious awards and lists in the field of children's literature), "Directory of Publishers," "Author Index," "Illustrator Index," "Subject Index," and "Title Index."

LISTING OF LIBRARY CONTACT INFORMATION

- Library of Congress **http://lcweb.loc.gov/**

- The American Library Association (ALA) **http://www.ala.org/**

- LII (Librarians' Index to the Internet—by Librarians, for Everyone) **http://www.lii.org/search/file/about**

This is an annotated, searchable subject directory of more than 7,600 Internet resources that have been evaluated by librarians for their usefulness to library users. It is helpful to both librarians and nonlibrarians.

- LIBWEB—Library Servers via the WWW **http://sunsite.berkeley.edu/Libweb/**

This site updates daily and lists over 6,100 pages from libraries in more than 100 countries. It is an excellent resource for getting to U.S. libraries on the WWW.

- Libraries on the Web—USA National **http://sunsite.berkeley.edu/Libweb/usa-org.html**

My favorite source for searching the WWW for Local Library Internet Access is **http://www.dogpile.com** which uses multiple search engines. I search for local libraries by entering the name of the state—for example, "Louisiana libraries."

Some Favorite Multicultural Children's Books

Aardema, Verna. *Bringing the Rain to Kapiti Plain*. New York: Scholastic, 1981. [A Nandi tale retold by Verna Aardema. Illustrated by Beatriz Vidal.] (ISBN: 0-590-72454-1) {Big book format}

Adoff, Arnold. *Black is brown is tan*. New York: HarperTrophy, 1973. [Illustrated by Emily Arnold McCully] (ISBN: 0-06-020083-9) {Winner of the NCTE Award for Excellence in Poetry for Children}

Adoff, Arnold. *In for Winter, Out for Spring*. San Diego: Harcourt Brace & Company, 1991. [Illustrated by Jerry Pinkney] (ISBN: 0-15-201492-6)

Baylor, Byrd. *I'm in Charge of Celebrations*. New York: Charles Scribner's Sons, 1986. [Illustrated by Peter Parnall] (ISBN: 0-684-185-79-2)

Brandt, Keith. *Rosa Parks: Fight for Freedom*. Mahwah, NJ: Troll Associates, 1993. [Illustrated by Gershom Griffith] (ISBN: 0-8167-2832-1)

Brightman, Alan. *Like Me*. Boston: Little, Brown and Company, 1976. [Photographs by Alan Brightman] (ISBN: 0-316-10808-1)

Bunting, Eve. *Smoky Night*. San Diego: Harcourt Brace & Company, 1994. [Illustrated by David Diaz] (ISBN: 0-15-269954-6) {Caldecott Medal winner}

dePaola, Tomie. *My First Chanukah*. New York: G. P. Putnam's Sons, 1989. [Illustrated by Tomie dePaola] (ISBN: 0-399-21780-0)

Feelings, Muriel. *Jambo means hello: Swahili Alphabet Book*. New York: Puffin Pied Piper, 1974. [Illustrated by Tom Feelings] (ISBN: 0-14-054652-9) {Caldecott Honor Book 1975} {ALA Notable Book, 1974} {Boston Globe/Horn Book Award for Illustration, 1974} {School Library Journal's Best Books of 1974} {Winner, Biennial of Illustrations, Bratislava, 1974} {Kirkus Choice, 1974} {IRA-CBC Children's Choices, 1974} {AIGA Bias-Free Illustration Show, 1975} {Child Study Association Books of the Year, 1974}

Feelings, Muriel. *Zamani Goes to Market*. Boston: Houghton Mifflin Company, 1970. [Illustrated by Tom Feelings] (ISBN: Not Given)

Flournoy, Valerie. *The Patchwork Quilt*. Dial Books for Young Readers, 1985. [Illustrated by Jerry Pinkney] (ISBN: 0-8037-0097-0) {Coretta Scott King Award Winner} {A Reading Rainbow Book}

Flournoy, Valerie. *Tanya's Reunion: A Sequel to The Patchwork Quilt*. Dial Books for Young Readers, 1985. [Illustrated by Jerry Pinkney] (ISBN: 0-8037-164-4)

Greenfield, Eloise. *Honey, I Love*. New York: HarperFestival, 1978/1995. [Illustrated by Jan Spivey Gilchrist] (ISBN: 0-694-00579-7)

Greenfield, Eloise. *Honey, I Love and Other Love Poems*. New York: HarperCollins, 1978. [Illustrated by Diane and Leo Dillon] (ISBN: 0-06-443097-9) {An ALA Notable Children's Book} {A Reading Rainbow Book}

Greenfield, Eloise. *She Come Bringing Me That Little Baby Girl*. New York: HarperCollins, 1974. [Illustrated by John Steptoe] (ISBN: 0-06-443296-3)

Hayes, Joe. *Antonio's Lucky Day: A Folktale from Mexico*. New York: Scholastic, 1993. [Retold by Joe Hayes. Illustrated by Oki S. Han.] (ISBN: 0-590-72882-2) {Big book format}

Hayes, Joe. *Coyote and the Butterflies: A Pueblo Indian Tale*. New York: Scholastic, 1993. [Retold by Joe Hayes. Adapted by Joseph Bruchac. Illustrated by Theresa Smith.] (ISBN: 0-590-72881-4) {Big book format}

Hoffman, Mary. *Amazing Grace*. New York: Dial Books for Young Readers, 1991. [Illustrated by Caroline Binch] (ISBN: 0-8037-1040-2) {A Reading Rainbow Book} {A Public Television Storytime Book}

Houston, Gloria. *My Great-Aunt Arizona*. New York: HarperCollins, 1992. [Illustrated by Susan Condie Lamb] (ISBN: 0-06-022606-4)

Joosse, Barbara M. *Mama, Do You Love Me?* New York: Scholastic, 1991. [Illustrated by Barbara Lavallee] (ISBN: 0-590-72752-4) {Big book format}

Keats, Ezra Jack. *Goggles!* New York: Scholastic, 1969. [Illustrated by Ezra Jack Keats] (ISBN: 0-439-11424-1) {Caldecott Honor Book}

Keats, Ezra Jack. *Peter's Chair*. New York: Scholastic, 1967. [Illustrated by Ezra Jack Keats] (ISBN: 0-439-11425-X)

Keats, Ezra Jack. *Whistle for Willie*. New York: Scholastic, 1964. [Illustrated by Ezra Jack Keats] (ISBN: 0-439-11423-3)

Lester, Julius. *Black Cowboy, Wild Horses: A True Story*. New York: Dial Books, 1998. [Illustrated by Jerry Pinkney] (ISBN: 0-8037-1787-3)

Lester, Julius. *John Henry*. New York: Dial Books for Young Readers, 1994. [Illustrated by Jerry Pinkney] (ISBN: 0-8037-1606-0) {A Caldecott Honor Book}

Paley, Vivian Gussin. *Boys & Girls: Superheroes in the Doll Corner*. Chicago: The University of Chicago Press, 1984. (ISBN: 0-266-64492-8)

Paley, Vivian Gussin. *The Girl with the Brown Crayon*. Cambridge, MA: Harvard University Press, 1997. (ISBN: 0-674-35442-7)

Paley, Vivian Gussin. *Kwanzaa and Me*. Cambridge, MA: Harvard University Press, 1995. (ISBN: 0-674-50586-7)

Paley, Vivian Gussin. (1981). *Wally's Stories: Conversations in the Kindergarten*. Cambridge, MA: Harvard University Press. (ISBN: 0-674-94593-X)

Paley, Vivian Gussin. *White Teacher*. Cambridge, MA: Harvard University Press, 1979/2000. (ISBN: 0-674-00273-3)

Pellegrini, Nina. *Families Are Different*. New York: Scholastic, 1991. [Illustrated by Nina Pellegrini] (ISBN: 0-590-72825-3) {Big book format}

Pfister, Marcus. *The Rainbow Fish*. (Translated by J. Alison James.) New York: North-South Books, 1992. [Illustrated by Marcus Pfister] (ISBN: 1-55858-009-3) {A 1993 Christopher Award Winner} {Winner of the 1993 Bologna Book Fair Critici in Erba Prize} {An IRA-CBC Children's Choice in 1993} {American Book Sellers Book of the Year for 1995}

Pinkney, Gloria Jean. *The Sunday Outing*. New York: Dial Books for Young Readers, 1994. [Illustrated by Jerry Pinkney] (ISBN: 0-8037-1198-0)

Polacco, Patricia. *Thunder Cake*. New York: Philomel Books, 1990. [Illustrated by Patricia Polacco] (ISBN: 0-399-22231-6)

Rylant, Cynthia. *When I Was Young in the Mountains*. New York: E. P. Dutton, 1992. [Illustrated by Diane Goode] (ISBN: 0-1405-4875-0)

San Souci, Robert D. *The Hired Hand: An African-American Folktale*. New York: Dial Books for Young Readers, 1997. [Illustrated by Jerry Pinkney] (ISBN: 0-8037-1296-0)

San Souci, Robert D. *The Talking Eggs: A Folktale from the American South*. New York: DialBooks for Young Readers, 1989. [Illustrated by Jerry Pinkney] (ISBN: 0-8037-0619-7){Caldecott Honor Book} {Coretta Scott King Award Honor Book}

Schroeder, Alan. *Minty: A Story of Young Harriet Tubman*. New York: Dial Books for Young Readers, 1996. [Illustrated by Jerry Pinkney] (ISBN: 0-8037-1888-8) {Coretta Scott King Award Winner} {An ALA Notable Book}

Walker, Barbara K. *The Most Beautiful Thing in the World: A Folktale from China*. New York: Scholastic, 1993. [Retold by Barbara K. Walker. Illustrated by Jean and Mou-sien Tseng.] (ISBN: 0-590-72883-0) {Big book format}

Whiteley, Opal. *Only Opal: The Diary of a Young Girl*. (Selections by Jane Boulton) New York: Scholastic, 1994. [Illustrated by Barbara Cooney] (ISBN: 0-590-53881-0) {Caldecott Honor Book} {A Reading Rainbow Book}

Williams, Vera B. *"More, More, More,"Said the Baby: 3 Love Stories*. New York: A Mulberry Paperback Book, 1990. [Illustrated by Vera B. Williams] (ISBN: 0-688-15634-7) {Caldecott Honor Book}

INTERNET RESOURCE (LOUISIANA CULTURE/LITERATURE):

Louisiana's Living Traditions (Virtual Books)
http://www.crt.state.la.us/folklife/creole_books_swapping_sto.html

This Internet site is a wonderful resource for teachers and children who want to learn more about Louisiana culture and literature. This particular site gives a quick history of the Louisiana Storytelling Project and lists excerpts from the publication *Swapping Stories: Folktales from Louisiana* (Online Resources), available to Internet users. Ten of the stories on the Louisiana Public Broadcasting server have video or audio clips. I suggest visiting this web site before going directly to the stories. Other excellent resources for more historical and cultural information about Louisiana are "INFO**louisiana**" **http://www.state.la.us/ed_students.htm** and **"Louisiana Voices" http://www.crt.state.la.us/folklife.**

Swapping Stories: Louisiana's Traditional Cultures
http://www.lpb.org/programs/swappingstories/cultures.html

The cultural diversity of Louisiana is of such magnitude that most "outsiders" can not fathom it! In an excerpt from *Swapping Stories: Folktales from Louisiana*, Maida Owens shares background information about the three main cultural regions of the state: New Orleans, South Louisiana, and North Louisiana. After reading this information, teachers may enjoy sharing with their classes the stories, retold by storytellers of the state. (Access stories by double clicking on "The Stories.")

VIRGINIA'S STAINED GLASS CANDY

Ingredients:

    1 box (16 oz.) confectioners' (powdered) sugar

    1 package (12 oz.) semisweet chocolate chips

    1 stick margarine

    1 package (10½ oz.) miniature marshmallows (pink, yellow, and green only*)

    1 cup chopped pecans

Directions:

1.   Cut off 3 sheets of aluminum foil (each approximately 18" long) and set aside.

2.   Spread 3 sheets of wax paper (each approximately 18" long) on a flat surface.

3.   Sift a row of powdered sugar (about 4" wide) down the center of each sheet of wax paper. Set aside sugared wax paper.

4.   Melt chocolate chips and margarine.

5.   Remove from heat and cool slightly.

6.   Stir in marshmallows and nuts.

7.   Spoon one third of the mixture in a log shape on the powdered sugar on each piece of wax paper.

8.   Sprinkle each log with more powdered sugar.

9.   Using your hands, roll each log separately until it is about 10" long and about 2" in diameter.

10.   Sprinkle again with powdered sugar so all surfaces are covered.

11.   Fold over the ends of the wax paper and roll up the candy log.

12.   Place each log diagonally on a separate piece of the aluminum foil.

13.   Turn the ends of the foil over the ends of each wax paper-covered log and roll up in the foil.

15.   Chill at least 2 hours. (May be frozen.)

16.   Cut into ½" slices before serving. (Makes approximately 60 pieces.)

*Note: The packages of marshmallows with these colors seem to have a better taste and appearance in this particular candy.

INDEXES

INDEX TO CHILDREN'S LITERATURE BY AUTHOR

INDEX TO CHILDREN'S LITERATURE BY ILLUSTRATOR

INDEX